MW01026411

Souvenir Portraits

Souvenir Portraits

❦

Paris in the Belle Epoque

JEAN COCTEAU

Translated by
Jesse Browner

Robson Books

First published in Great Britain in 1991 by
Robson Books Ltd, Bolsover House, 5 – 6
Clipstone Street, London W1P 7EB

Copyright © 1990 Paragon House
The right of Paragon House to be identified as
author of this work has been asserted by them in
accordance with the Copyright, Designs and
Patents Act 1988

Originally published in French under the title *Portraits souvenir.*
Copyright © Editions Bernard Grasset, 1935.

British Library Cataloguing in Publication Data
Cocteau, Jean *1889 – 1963*
    Souvenir portraits : Paris in the Belle Epoque.
    1. France. Paris. Social life, history
    I. Title II. (Portraits – souvenir) *English*
    944.36

    ISBN 0 86051 710 1

Printed in Great Britain by Billing & Sons Ltd,
Worcester

Jean Cocteau
Souvenir Portraits

Jean Cocteau was born at Maisons-Laffitte on July 5, 1889. His father died when Cocteau was ten years old, and he was raised by his mother and his maternal grandfather, a cosmopolitan patron of the arts at whose home he would meet the celebrities of the day. After undistinguished studies at the Lycée Condorcet, he found his vocation as a poet, and in 1908 his friend, the actor Edouard de Max, organized a recital to bring him to society's attention. Momentarily intoxicated by his easily-won success, Cocteau was drawn into the circle of Anna de Noailles, Lucien Daudet, and the Rostands, who would hail him as a child prodigy. But his encounter with the *ballets russes* and such masters of the avant-garde as Diaghilev and Stravinsky led him to renounce his fashionable fame and to disclaim the poems with which he had earned it.

In the 1920s began the most fertile and tormented period of Cocteau's life. He wrote plays (*Les Mariés de la Tour Eiffel, Antigone*); poetry (*Le Cap de Bonne-Espérance*); and novels (*Thomas L'imposteur, Les Enfants Terribles*). In 1922, the death of his friend Raymond Radiguet plunged him into a deep depression. He reasserted his catholic faith under the influence of Jacques Maritain, but soon abandoned his mystical inclinations for drugs as a palliative to his grief. In 1929 he underwent his final detoxification treatment, during which he would write *Les Enfants Terribles* in seventeen days.

In 1930, Cocteau directed his first film, *Le Sang D'un Poète,* a surrealist short that caused a *scandale.* The same year, his play *La Voix Humaine* was performed at the Comédie-Française. From then until 1946, Cocteau concentrated mostly on playwriting, producing *La Machine Infernale* (1934), *Les Parents Terribles* (1938), *Renaud et Armide* (1943), and *L'Aigle à Deux Têtes* (1935); but he also published *Portraits-Souvenir* (1935) and *Mon Premier Voyage,* the account of a voyage around the world in eighty days undertaken on a wager.

Cocteau would continue to exploit every form of artistic expression for the rest of his life, adapting some of his plays for the screen, *Les Parents Terribles* and *L'Aigle à Deux Têtes,* while pursuing his poetic writing, *Allégorie* (1941), *Clair-Obscur* (1954), and *Requiem* (1962), as well as his prose work, *La Difficulté D'être* (1947), *Le Journal d'un Inconnu* (1952). Cocteau died at his home in Milly-la-Forêt on October 11, 1963.

Cocteau was forty-six when he published *Portraits-Souvenir.* Still too young to write his memoirs—a task he would continue to avoid—he was yet old enough to evoke that literary, artistic, and social Paris that vanished in 1914, and whose landscapes blend with those of his own youth.

*"I am a liar
who always tells the truth."*

—J.C. (*Opéra*)

Contents

Introduction

What, exactly, are souvenir portraits? They are the photographs one has taken at the top of the Eiffel Tower or at a fairground, where "the customer passes his head through an enormous painted collar, which transports him from his everyday life to the cockpit of a biplane or perches him in a Serpollet automobile or a boxing ring." In other words, the portraits and places depicted in the essays function as quaint relics, nostalgic snapshots which, in their own way, are ideal vehicles for transporting us into another time, another place, where we ourselves were quite different and our old friends and acquaintances were still alive.

And Cocteau does indeed transport us there—although by the time he comes to write of them, most of these people (actors, writers, musicians, aristocrats) and the prewar Europe they embodied have long been dead. One by one, he resurrects the inhabitants of his carefree youth, the days when he was still the "Frivolous Prince" dancing through the salons, enchanting his elders with the facility of his wit, the precocious sophistication of his verse, and the elegance of his lovely hands.

Here is a parade of figures historical and not so, marching, as Cocteau would have it, to phantom drums. Some of the names will be familiar to any modern reader—Sarah Bernhardt, Colette, Empress Eugénie. Others, such as the actor Edouard de Max, the poet Anna de Noailles, Catulle Mendès, or the schoolboy Dargelos, may be familiar only to a more specialized readership. None of this matters in the slightest—the portrait is the thing; the shadow, in Cocteau's hand, becomes the substance, and the Belle Époque dandies and cocottes live on.

But the souvenir portrait is something else as well. The primary meaning of the French word *souvenir* is not "souvenir" but "recollection" or "memory." Thus, *Portraits-Souvenir* might be equally if loosely translated as "Portraits from Memory," and it is precisely the quality of that memory, the wealth and focus of detail it has retained, that inform us most eloquently about the young salon poet. In other words, the souvenir portraits together make up a composite portrait of the poet himself, a portrait that is a memory of what he once was in a bygone age. Here is Cocteau the enigmatic fashion plate in Polaire, the flamboyant father figure to wayward boys in de Max; here is Cocteau the whimsical exhibitionist in Sarah Bernhardt, the patriarch of letters in Mendès, the earthy iconoclast in Mistinguett; here is Cocteau the dignified ambassador of a lost age in the Empress Eugénie, the artist-clown, the holy buffoon, in Footit. Can we wonder that he is so indulgent to their foibles and failings, or so extravagant in his praise of their genius? They are all a part of him—they are all him. In remembering himself as a boy, Cocteau is recreating in his own image the world he inhabited.

Likewise, in the guise of depiction, we encounter the same obsessive themes that run throughout Cocteau's autobiographical musings: the "poet as medium," fashion, angels, childhood infatuation, the precision of poetry, the subtle digs at André Gide. Even the schoolboy Dargelos, a semimythical figure whose presence haunts most of Cocteau's important works, makes his appearance among the immortals, "the archetype of all that cannot be learned, taught, judged, punished"—a succinct encapsulation of Cocteau's vision of *himself.*

If we consider that in 1935 Cocteau was struggling desperately against his addiction to opium, then the golden hue, the sometimes weepy nostalgia, and the soft focus that inform the portraits become simultaneously more understandable and more telling. Who, looking back from the vantage point of the grey, totalitarian thirties, would not tend to deify the whimsical, flitting pixies of the art nouveau decade? How, in the dark corner of an opium-suffused room, could the memory of Anna de Noailles fail to conjure up visions of a nightingale rehearsing to the starlit night? How could Rossini's head emerging from the sheets be anything but a "monumental egg" to a frightened child? How could Colette, in 1935 already a venerable *grande dame* of sixty-two, fail to be rejuvenated as anything but a "little fox in a cyclist's outfit, a fox terrier in skirts?" And how, finally, should Cocteau, in his advancing middle age with the world darkening around him, have banished from his head the soothing echoes of the "laughter that will never be laughed again?"

As Margaret Crosland points out, ". . . with Cocteau everything is theatrical . . . for him, life has always appeared a statement in theatrical terms."* Indeed, every souvenir portrait seems here to be a performer, each one a soloist pirouetting endlessly in his or her own private spotlight, indifferent and unaffected by the passage of time. They are all acts in Cocteau's circus, and circus performers, especially for an eternal child, are always somehow superhuman. Like the acrobats at the circus, the portraits are irradiated by that "golden, powdered manure . . . that hangs rainbows on the light bulbs and glory on the acrobats' work." It is the powder that has fertilized the imagination and memory of the greatest of all the acrobats he depicts—Cocteau himself.

Jesse Browner

*Introduction to Jean Cocteau, *My Contemporaries,* Margaret Crosland ed., trans., Chilton Book Co.: Philadelphia, 1968.

Souvenir Portraits

1

The undesirable.—Poets get nothing but love letters.—Fits and starts.—Figaro.

Writing memoirs seems to me to be an impossible task. First of all, I get my periods confused. I sometimes leap ten years forward and place people in surroundings that belong to others. Memory is a dim and appalling night. I would fear to venture into it at the risk of incurring the punishment of those archeologists who desecrate Egyptian sepulchers. Tombs avenge themselves. There is a type of sleep that rejects the sacrilege of light and calls down curses. No, it would doubtless be more reasonable and less morbid to play at cockshy in reverse: that is to say, to use the ball to resurrect the event instead of knocking it down, and to aim in such a way that a figure emerges from the shadows, bearing certain places and circumstances strung about it, like the managers in *Parade,*[1] whom Picasso clothed in skylines of Paris and New York.

Such costumes are commonly found in the stalls of fairground photographers. The customer passes his head through an enormous painted collar, which transports him from his everyday life to the cockpit of a biplane or perches him in a Serpollet automobile or a boxing ring. The "souvenir portraits" that I should like to offer would be peculiar in that the customer would furnish his own illusion, thus preventing me from confusing my dates and settings—a confusion that adds to the charm of those whimsical fairground effigies, but which would ill serve my search for precision.

The poet is the vehicle, the natural medium of unknown forces that manipulate him, taking advantage of his purity to broadcast themselves throughout the world and, if not to resolve, at least to emphasize *ad nauseam* the problems we all try to avoid from the moment we wake up. Scarcely have we opened our eyes of a morning, after the awful muddle of dreaming, than we attempt to forget an order of things in which the poet specializes, and which makes him the very model of the *undesirable*. Now, of all the grievances laid at his feet, isn't that of precision one of the most unfair? The poet is precise. Poetry is precision. Since Baudelaire, the public has gradually come to understand that poetry is one of the most insolent ways of stating the truth. There is no weapon more precise, and it is in order to defend themselves, through a survival instinct that fears precision and revelatory insights that the masses insist on confusing poetry with mendacity, quick-wittedness with paradox.

What is the use of telling a story that does not carry the inimitable weight of truth? What good are imaginary memoirs, falsified anecdotes, words put in the wrong mouths, picturesque recollections? One is crippled with exhaustion under the dead weight of imprecision. A floodlight's beam is altogether different, wandering over the surface of the night amassed behind each of us, focusing on some meaningful face, some actor or place, so as to give it the maximum of expressive force, to resurrect it.

(N)

Souvenir Portraits. I should like to collect my souvenir portraits by fits and starts. By that I mean that the starts, which would be events in chronological order, would appear fitful through the distorting element of memory, but would in fact be fitful in appearance only. I might thus have found a more vital and less pretentious method of ransacking the void.

Poets only possess intimate memoirs. There is no secretary capable of answering the strange messages and written cries addressed to the poet by unknown friends in distant rooms, friends whom his books have recruited and who, in the final analysis, are the only excuse for writing; I might add that poets walk slightly above the ground, on a snow that has soon melted and borne away their footprints. This all makes it rather awkward to remember and to clothe one's ghosts in flesh. In the dangerous game of turning back towards the blazing past, one runs the risk of being turned into a pillar of salt, which is to say a pillar of tears.

1934–1935. A curtain falls, a curtain rises. Life is dead, long live life! Dead is an age that I lived to the full, grudgingly and with all my heart; about to start is a new age that my antennae have detected, an age in which I perceive nobility and whose portents are good. I take advantage of a minute's intermission to rise, stretch, look around, and take my opera glasses for a stroll.

I have known many singular people and places whom I distinguish from the plural mass and who inhabit me without taking an active part in the concerns that guide me and mark my way. What strikes me most about these stars in the Parisian firmament, these sacred monsters (places or people), is that their originality of appearance—what distinguished them from others, gave them some dimension, spotlit them—stemmed less from an effort to set themselves apart than from a struggle against death, and that their pathetic struggles magnified them, created between them and mere caricatures the same difference that exists between the gentleman who takes little steps with a Japanese parasol in his hand and the acrobat who executes the same steps, brandishing the same parasol, on a tightrope.

In short, I only retain the memory of characters and settings that thirsted for survival, whose frivolity depended on tragedy, whose lightfootedness had something of the prodigious and whose silhouettes, in the words of Thomas Mann's masterpiece *The Magic Mountain,* were silhouettes "in enlarged format."

@

Souvenir portraits in enlarged format. Now there's a journalistic undertaking that I find tempting. Am I up to it? The main thing is to hinder nothing in advance, not to parcel out a volume in little slices, but to throw oneself headfirst into the night.

For I do not approve of the mixing of genres: a play must be a play, a film a film, a novel a novel, an article an article.

One day, as I was reading a poison-pen letter to Picasso, he said: "It's an anonymous letter," and when I showed him that it was signed, he added: *"That makes no difference. The anonymous letter is a genre."* That's why I composed a spoken song.* Song is a genre. Whether it be sung or recited, it bears reference neither to monologue nor to poetry: it remains a song. An article is a genre. It must resemble nothing else.

An article for the Saturday *Figaro,* an article by a poet recalling his life, I see as something light, fleet, written in fresh ink at the edge of an editorial desk, without any touching up or any relation to the politics of literature, at the surface of the age and of the ages, taking part in the laughter that has honored all solemn minds and that splits a man down the middle to his very heart.

And just as false solemnity alone rejects laughter, so, too, do false *grandes époques* scorn the lightheartedness, the heady froth, the supreme elegance of the high and tragic eras.

Shall I confess? This new era, the new age that I foresee, gives me great hope and excites me immensely. Had I youth and fortune, I would cross the place Vendôme tomorrow in a dashing buggy; via the Concorde and the Champs-Elysées, I would reach the offices of the newspaper whose steps George Sand used to climb as a young dandy, a cigar clenched between her teeth; and I would strive to resemble Amy Boisseau's charming colossus, that Barber of Seville who guards the entrance, a bronze guitar slung across his shoulder. Covered in bronze frills and bronze pompoms, he trims the bronze barbs of his bronze quill, which he keeps well sharpened with a bronze razor.

* *Anna la bonne.*

2

The Vaudeville and the Pavillon de Hanovre.—Réjane's mules.—Rossini's house.—Sarasate.

The Paramount is the ghost of the Vaudeville. At the scene of the crime, on the spot where that queen of the concert halls died, burnt alive by commerce, at the corner of the boulevard where that red, golden, and beloved heart of the Paris of my childhood beats, on that macadam at the edge of which one could see the mules of Réjane's cab in attendance, the Paramount rears its head day and night, lunar and hideous, with its enormous talking specters and its orchestra rising from the depths. The Parisian hurries by, crossing himself. He misses that paragon of concert halls, one of the three or four that, by some happy stroke of fate, had that something which cannot be purposely achieved, and which ought to be protected like the trees of the public gardens, the lungs of a capital. Other than the official theaters, there remain only Les Variétés, L'Ambigu, Le Gymnase, and Les Bouffes.

If young people are to understand the lost glory of the old Vaudeville, I advise them to go hear Madame

My recollection of Réjane

Pitoëff, before her husband is compelled to cut short the exhausting sacrifice to which she is condemned by her role in *Tonight We Improvise*.* To her children in their nightshirts, she speaks of the Theater. I do not believe that there exists a more fervent plea for those old halls, sorely beset by the modern taste for necropolises.

A ravishing little death's head delicately balanced on a sort of odd, scarecrow's body in a long, black gown that would scare anything alive except a bird, Madame Pitoëff mimics the great heroines of the footlights. She evokes the chandeliers, the boxes, the elegant half-light and the painted cloth of the tall curtains rising on the sun of drama.

The curtain of the classical matinees at the Comédie-Française, the anticipation of the three funereal knocks of *Oedipus Rex,* the glow of the curtain at the Châtelet, its mica monocle, the figures-of-eight made by the proscenium sprinkler, the girl selling caramels during intermission, the orchestra striking up the prelude: a host of memories pours through us as we watch the actress losing all reserve and consuming herself in the very fire of professional hell.

Since I'm writing by fits and starts, another hall the thought of whose destruction makes me tremble in fear is the little theater of the Conservatoire. My grandfather had his reserved seats in the third row in the orchestra on the right. There, in that sarcophagus of painted wood peopled with venerable mummies, I dis-

* Pirandello.

covered Beethoven, Liszt, Berlioz, and Wagner in quick and jumbled succession. It was some kind of miracle, that hall! But if the curtain, that light scarlet wall, the abrupt footlights, the flaming sword of the archangel on the threshold of paradise, were wasted on my childish imagination, what grabbed it were the tiers of seats, the shameless commotion of the chorus members in beards, binoculars, *princesse* gowns, yellow bows on their shoulders, black velvet ribbons around their necks, as they settled in, jabbering before the organ blast cruelly prolonged by the conductor to the very last cough, until that poor, myopic lady, crushed with embarrassment, managed at last to find her seat and sit down in it.

The Vaudeville, the dear old Vaudeville which I saw demolished, assassinated (like the Pavillon de Hanovre across the street, whose ghost of grottoes, mazes, aquariums, Mickey Mouse, bird cages, mercury globes and nautical games is no less unsettling than the ghostly Paramount)—my mother, as a little girl, saw it go up over the ruins of the Rue Basse-du-Rempart. My grandparents lived opposite, on the Rue de la Chaussée-d'Antin, on the fourth floor, across the hall from Winterhalter. On the second floor of the same building lived the Rossinis. The Rossinis received many eminent gentlemen and beautiful ladies, and Madame Rossini—who, like Madame Fenouillard visiting the Sioux, could not abide tobacco—would send the "gentlemen" up to the fourth floor to smoke. For her part, my grandmother tolerated the smell of stale tobacco out of love for music. Madame Rossini was a dry and nasty woman. Were she offered some *foie gras*, at supper with the Gustave de Rothschilds, she would push it away, saying, "Thank you, I do not eat animals' diseases," and she would crush crackers on the table-cloth with her lorgnette for her little toothless dog. Rossini terrified my mother. My grandfather would shove her into his bedroom of a morning, bearing a basket of eggs. She would see, resting on a piano, a row of wigs destined for that monumental egg emerging from the sheets and eiderdowns. The wigs, displayed on racks, ranged from long-haired to short-haired. The master tried them on, one after another, until the ficti-tious visit from the hairdresser.

One of those wigs, in its green, oval box, became one of the fetishes of my childhood, the object of covert searches in my grandfather's dressing room, begun the moment the quartet brought me proof that he wouldn't catch me in there and that I could rummage at my leisure. For those quartets, the aura of the Rossinis, the musical atmosphere of that building where I never went was extended to 45, Rue la Bruyère, the town-house where we lived throughout my childhood. The courtyard of the two-storied house overlooked the Gaveau gardens (more music!). My grandparents lived on the upper floor, in an apartment which the archi-tect's whim had set out in such a way that one had to walk down corridors, climb and descend steep stair-ways, to go from one room to another. An apartment perfectly adapted to the free-for-alls and fantasies of childhood. By dint of embedding and complicating its layout in my dreams, I am no longer able to put it in its true place. It has left the building, cast off and floated

Saluts à ma grand-mère

Bowing to my grandmother

away like an airship. I remember an apartment and
rooms belonging to us, and far, far away, in another
world, in some unreal and fabulous region, the apartment where my grandfather had a silver bathtub that
rang like a gong, an apartment full of shoes and books
where he collected Greek busts, Ingres drawings,

le Corset "droit
a maisons laffitte

The straight corset at Maisons-Laffitte

Delacroix paintings, Florentine medallions, ministers'
manuscripts, Antinous masks, vases from Cyprus, and
Stradivariuses.

My preference was for the cases which held the
masks and violins. Behind the glass, the Antinous
masks with their enamel eyes, their pale, terracotta
cheeks and bearded collars, lounged in red velvet as if in
a theater box by Manet. The violins adorned the billiards room. They were bedded down in the royal blue
jewel cases of ebony chests whose drawers contained
rosin, strings, chanterelles, and billiard chalk. For these
instruments were used. Even the sacred Stradivariuses,
which hum whenever one of their kind is played any-
where else (*sic*), abandoned the blue velvet on the
nights when the quartet gathered: Sarasate,[1] Sivori,
Grébert, and the music-loving host, Eugène Lecomte.
On those evenings of chamber music, the game for my
cousins and me consisted of creeping along the solemn
staircase that connected the two floors. Through
the witchcraft that had removed the upper apartment
from space, the game, I repeat, made that stairway a
place in itself, self-sufficient, whose uppermost limit
was the gate set up by my grandfather to keep us from
falling.

The game, then, consisted of waiting for Sarasate
to arrive, all of us hidden behind a halberd-lamp of
crimson plush that we used in our "poor prisoner"
game, and of taking the opportunity of his stopping
before the antechamber mirror to adjust his hair, to
close the gate, and thus complete the *tableau* of the
"Caged Lion-Tamer."

With his fat whiskers, his grey mane, his frogged
frock-coat, his watch chains, his trousers with their

de fiacre des virtuoses

The carriage of the virtuosi

footstraps, and his little varnished boots, we thought that Sarasate, behind the gate, looked like a lion dressed as a tamer, which satisfied a thirst in us for cartoons and high caricature before they existed.

Otherwise, the real spectacle, the ultimate game of the *tableaux,* was our vacations at Maisons-Laffitte. The chateau of Maisons-Laffitte adorns a vast park of lindens, lawns, flower beds, fountains, white fences, tennis courts, horse races, cyclists, and middle-class proprieties. There, I would pedal furiously as far as the Saint-Germain forest, to smoke revolting snuff in secret with Aimé Simon-Girard, using horse chestnuts hollowed into pipe bowls with a penknife and held with an elder twig. Afterwards, we would get down on all fours and graze, so as not to smell of tobacco.

The trainers led the high life. Max Lebaudy, the "little sugar bowl," washed his barouches with champagne and organized bullfights. One might see Madame du Gast, the president of the Society for the Prevention of Cruelty to Animals, led away by guardians of the peace. There were gymkhanas with sack races and ladies out walking with beribboned rabbits on leashes.

On Sundays, from dawn onwards, my grandfather, dressed in a tussore jacket, his straw hat tipped back, and carrying a little bouquet of primroses, waited on the Place Sully, which was graced in the middle with a gaslight and a bed of begonias, and watched the avenues leading up from the race track. Suddenly, beneath a merciless sun, the virtuosi arrived. They came in an open hackney, without a coachman. The carriage of Fantômas[2] rolling along, guided by the dead. The carriage of the virtuosi! Melpomene[3] or some instrumental allegory surely presided, invisible, at the helm.

Sarasate, his right foot on his left knee, shoulders sunk into the rear cushions, wearing an opera hat, jacket, and gloves all of red leather, held the reins and drove the team from the back seat. As soon as they arrived at our house, the horses, mad with exhaustion, were unharnessed and fed a soup of hot burgundy and carrots, while the virtuosi took luncheon. Sivori was a midget. At the table, my grandmother sat him on musical scores. "Not on Beethoven, Madame!" he would cry, "not on Beethoven," spiking the strawberries with his toothpick. My grandfather cut his meat with the same gesture he would later use in attacking a musical phrase with his sporting bow. Yes, that chamber music was not music to be listened to and enjoyed, but to be executed, measured, tossed off by the leader. A sport, an exercise like any other—fencing, canoeing, boxing. Each person found in it what he wanted. It brought old friends together and prevented arguments between them, while assuring us of being able to ransack forbidden rooms with impunity and providing us with belly laughs and charades.

Grébert had the cello. Every time my grandmother passed by at the other end of the room, on tiptoe, her knitting in her hand, he would rise and greet her while continuing to play, bowing to the empty space.

After the quartet, our virtuosi disguised themselves as peasants and went to serenade the lady doctor, Madame Gache-Sarrothe, a neighbor of ours on the Place Sully and the inventor of the straight corset. Night was falling. The Big Dipper twinkled above the garden. The sprinkler system exalted the heliotrope. We dined, the children in a dining room designated for the "little outcasts," where my cousin refused to eat from anything but the china marked with Napoleon's crest. After dinner, the gentlemen seasoned their meerschaum pipes and Sarasate told of his triumphs in Europe. Dangling at the end of a chain, he had a little golden coffin that contained a tiny, realistic violin given him by the queen of Spain. One night, the tiny, realistic violin fell into a glass of beer. They tried to fish it out with a straw. At the center of the general commotion,

le violon de le rareine !

Sarasate tore at his hair and cried out, rolling his *r*'s, "*Le violon de la reine! Le violon de la reine!*"[4]

And these are moments without any other interest than that of revealing the angle from which childhood observes the adult world, piecemeal, on all fours, behind pantry doors and on the stairs, with an eye that absorbs only poetic intensity.

3

My mother dresses for the theater.—"La Grève des Forgerons."—The Lumière Brothers basement.—Old England.—Childhood recaptured.

The theater! Evenings at the Comédie-Française and evenings at the Opéra!

This is how things went. I was present at my mother's dressing. A cloud of perfume and mauve rice powder suffused the room, the twilight through the chintz curtains with multicolored prints (exotic trees and tropical birds). A door open on the bright gaslight of the dressing room lit up the mirrored wardrobe, which reflected the scene even more beautifully and profoundly. It was in that mirror that I followed the preparations. From my seat between the dressing table and the fireplace, my mother—slim, monumental and foreshortened—seemed to be held up by the long stiff dress in red velvet embroidered in jet, a Raudnitz dress with balloon sleeves from which her arms, shoulders and bosom rose, pale against a fringe of the same red velvet on a very simple bodice just right as the background of the classic scene at the edge of the loges: a

21

ma mère s'habille pour aller voir l'Énigme

My mother dresses to go see L'Énigme

fluttering fan of tortoise shell and black lace, the raising of a mother-of-pearl lorgnette, discrete applause. That, at least, was the pantomime I imagined during the ritual of the long gloves, dead skins so difficult to get into, that began to live, to cling and to take form with every successive effort of each individual finger, and the charming finale which consisted of buttoning at the wrist, with a feminine gesture immortalized by Mayol,[1] the little opening through which I kissed her naked palm. That marked the end of the show, the prologue to the real show for which all these refinements had been invented, and the wardrobe mirror showed me my mother—what am I saying, that madonna clad in velvet, strangled with diamonds, plumed in her nighttime aigrette, a sparkling chestnut bristling with rays of light, tall, listless, torn between the last admonitions to be good and the parting glances at the mirror. The chambermaid, prostrate, spreading out the train on her knees, was the final touch which conferred upon my mother the nobility of a Spanish Virgin.

Next, her fur coat concealing bouquets and shining bracelets, my mother leaned over, gave me a quick peck, and was off to that ocean of murmurs, jewels, feathers, and skulls, into which she would throw herself like a red river, to mingle her velvet with the velvet of the theater, her glitter with the glitter of the chandeliers and girandolas.

I dreamed of the theater. I had a hard time picturing it based on these departures and prefigurative likenesses. When my brother Paul was taken—to *Samson and Delilah*, if I'm not mistaken—I was somewhat consoled by the thought that one of us had set sail on the

My father and mother at the opera

red river and that perhaps my turn would come to sail on it and to see those great, forbidden halls of gold.

My mother and father went to the Comédie-Française or to the Opéra. On opera night, they would take the scores to *Meistersinger* or *Tannhaüser*. *La Grève des Forgerons* was playing at the Comédie-Française. Alone on stage, before a tribunal of shareholders who made their entrance in purple, ermine and toques, Mounet-Sully[2] declaimed that interminable poem which begins: "My story, Your Honors, will be brief." The memory and the glory of that monologue-play had no little influence over me when I decided to read *La Voix Humaine*[3] before the Reading Society of the Théatre Français.

La Grève was being performed with *L'Énigme,* by Paul Hervieu. I was familiar with *L'Énigme* through an exquisite caricature by Cappiello[4] published in the magazine *Le Théatre*. The hook-nosed, young owl's profile of the "divine" Madame Bartet and the horse-like profile of Marthe Brandès confront one another on a palace staircase. "Whose lover will he be?" In one hand, the ladies are carrying small globular lamps and in the other they grasp their dressing gowns, adorned with broderie anglaise and frills.

It was the era of problem plays, when Berthe Cerny dissimulated her agitation from Raphaël Duflos by standing up, bunching her skirt, extending her calf, and offering the sole of her right foot to the logs of an enormous fireplace. The grownups avoided discussing the problem of the play in our presence, and it was through the mediation of Cappiello's astonishing synthesis (his Japanese pencil endowed actresses, over and

scène d'amour
aux "Français"

Love scene at the "Français"

above a perfect likeness, with the beauty of flora and
fauna, of tigers and orchids) through the media of
tableside insinuations and postcards that my brother
kept hidden between the pages of his study books—
that I blended the plays into one single show, influ-
enced by the Guignol, the stairway on the Rue La

Bruyère, and mass at the Trinité.* This show furnished
intrigues, characters and fantastical scenery to the theaters I built from empty Old England boxes, theaters
that made me bless the stimulating fevers of the mea-
sles, scarlatina, and appendicitis.

Convalescence ended in the sunshine in the courtyard of no. 45. We hammered, we glued, we cut up, we
painted, we invented systems of candle-powered footlights and collapsible prompter's booths. My German
Josephine (my fräulein) sewed the costumes. The ma-
nia for building theaters in the courtyard, for decorating and lighting them, lasted up to my days at the
Lycée Condorcet, where, thanks to certain heaven-sent
gifts and to fraulein Joséphine, I ran away with all the
booby prizes—German, drawing, gymnastics—be-
littling by my ridiculous presence the podium of honor
and the Saint-Charlemagne[5] banquet.

René Rocher, my classmate, seconded my under-
takings. Now that he manages real theaters, he may
remember our courtyard at 45, Rue La Bruyère. The
mess piled up in the middle. A shed on the right furnished nails and planks—it was the old stable. Over
each empty stall one read the horse's name: Urchin,
Mascot. To the left, behind an ivy-covered wall, one
heard the water hose washing down the Comte and
Comtesse de Crèvecoeur's victoria.

My God, how few distractions there were in those
days! Childhood intoxicated us with uninterrupted
spectacle, but the poor grownups who hated staying at
home and did not possess our mysterious resources had
the choice between Yvette Guilbert, *La Marche à l'Etoile*

*Later, at the *Mercure,* I would come to know the wonderful
sarcasms of Rouveyre, who sprays his ink like a squid.

at the Théâtre d'Ombres Chinoises, Robert-Houdin, *Théodora* with Sarah Bernhardt, *Le Nouveau Jeu* with Lavallière, *La Citoyenne Cotillon* with Granier, *Le Duel* with Le Bargy, and Guitry in *L'Assommoir* (or some such program). And it was pleasant, and it was lasting, and there were no films, no dancing halls, and no real music halls.

The superb and resounding slaps that Françoise Rosay delivers to her godson in Feyder's film *Pension Mimosas* should be administered to the pessimists who never stop complaining: "There's nothing at the theater or at the cinema, nothing's happening, they give us nothing . . ." For where is that naive age when we saw *L'Arroseur arrosé, Le Bock,* and *Bébés au bord de l'eau* in the Lumière Brothers basement near Old England? (Old England, where they sold sailor's suits with whistles, putty-colored monkey jackets, and those wretched gaiters lined with red flannel that itches your legs, held a central place in our childhood.) Nowadays, the comfortable gloom is peopled by obedient ghosts with ringing voices, by alabaster statues who speak and act, by dead heroines, and Hokusai's[6] *Wave* looks like some dismal color cartoon that doesn't move. And without listing for you the theaters overflowing with works in which the genius of modern actors should suffice to put boredom to shame, I marvel at the innumerable amusements with which a city's beauty can gild its lily, and I listen, among others, to the thrilling troop of blonds, brunettes, and redheads who sing the love songs. Damia, Fréhel, Lucienne Boyer, Lys Gauty, Oswald . . . mightn't one think that your almost anonymous songs had been discovered by sorcerers, ready-made, famous already, and ready to erupt from the sidewalks of the capital?

Last Sunday, at the Pleyel, I was thinking about this wealth of major and minor entertainments, this mad prodigality of a city of genius in the face of so much ingratitude, when Serge Lifar[7] appeared between the vast curtains, wearing the bloody tunic of Apollon Musagète,[8] escorted by Russian specters, oiled in dramatic solitude and looking like a crime of passion.

I was thinking of him and Al Brown, and Greta Garbo, and all the stars of stage, ring, and screen, and even the models at a Chanel fashion show—models who might be compared to jockeys who are their own horses, turning in their mirrored paddocks—that they all live in some parallel fairyland, that in their actions they possess the secret resources of lightning and its appalling mischievousness, that the public mistrusts them as much as it does poets, that the masses adore them, despise them, and hang on their least stumble, and that, in order to enjoy them, one must cultivate and rediscover the childhood which poets extend to their deaths and which the city grownups boast of having lost.

4

*Refusing the medicine.—The little death.—
Mother Lachique's sack.—Le Châtelet.—
Around the World in Eighty Days.—A cynical
little girl.—Cosima Wagner and Offenbach.*

I wish to be read by people who have remained
children at any cost. I can tell them a mile away. A look
into the primitive fairyland is better protection against
the ravages of age than any beauty treatment, any diet.
But alas, such people, who wish to live snugly curled up
in the refuge of that credulous fairyland as if in the
maternal womb, are wounded by our nervous age, by
its disorder, its restlessness, its twitching lights, its vehicles, its numerous pretexts to divide, to tear away from
others and from oneself.

The child wants a room where he can gather his
toys and his loves. He hates anything that scatters. He
prefers illnesses that group and cloister. I pushed this
phobia of departures, of places where one has a hard
time picturing one's loved ones, to an idolatry of
thunder. It is certainly because of that sweet bowling of
April thunder, that Sunday thunder that coos and rear-

ranges the furniture of the heavens, that I still retain my worship of it. That thunder was the sign that our plans for a walk would dissolve, the assurance that the family would stay at home, that my cousins would help me with my building blocks, that the nurses would sew in circles, that I would hear the quartet and, later, the billiard balls clicking below and testifying to the childishness of grownups.

Cursed were the circumstances that forced me, on Sundays, from my comfortable dreams and from my hole, that hole which the hermitess of Poitiers would one day call her "dear little cave," her "dear Malampia deeps." Cursed, with two exceptions: one arising from the discontent of grownups, the other from their content. Both of these exceptional cases prompted a little death, a little death game, an exquisite anxiety, incited, hoped for, hidden, feared, and extremely complex, in which the pride and shame of being rewarded or punished played no part. One prolonged the dream of Sundays in the country, the other of Sundays in town. These circumstances gave me rest, in a certain way, substituting for my personal enchantments fortuitous and unpredictable ones. Here is the first: a revolting cup in my right hand, a peppermint in my left, I refused my Sunday morning medicine. They pleaded, I refused; they insisted, I refused; they begged, I refused. Scarcely had the terrible glare in my mother's eyes betrayed the lie in her still soothing voice, and the slap grazed my cheek, than the little death was set in motion.

No matter how familiar I was with the ploy, the *little death* always arrived and took me by surprise. It took me on its shoulder in a sack. Pierre Barrère, my grandfather's bewhiskered servant (he ate live snails,

La mère Lachique m'emporte

Mother Lachique carries me off

32

crunching the shells between his teeth), disguised himself as Mother Lachique. After a brief, convincing scene, he threw me in the sack and ran from floor to floor, so as to disorient me and confuse my surroundings. I believed it all, I savored my terror. My heart beat, my mouth went dry, my ears hummed, and I emerged from the sack drunk on the gloom, the jolts, the dreaming, ready to refuse my medicine, having truly crossed the river of death and clutching in my hand, as my fare for the ferryman, a half-melted peppermint.

In town, the *little death* sprang from a reward: seats for a show! We were going to see a show! Barely had I heard the great news than the machinery started up. A dark, endless hallway, a little death hallway, was born in my feverish sleep, crossed through Sunday morning, and opened out into daylight opposite the "tribunal" of the ticket collectors and the judges in black of a matinee at the Châtelet or the Nouveau Cirque.

La Biche au Bois, Around the World. First shows! First deliria! Later, when we know the wings, the actors, the directors, when the newspapers and our work have drawn us into the scene, being in the theater is finished for us. We may think we're there, but it's finished! Never can Tristram's dying plaint, as he looks out across the sea, usurp the place held in our soul by Philéas Fogg's "20,000 dollars for you, Captain, if we reach Liverpool tonight!" and never can the scenery of the Ballet Russe bequeath us such a memory as that of the enchanted snows where the Indian chief unhitched the locomotive.

❦

Philéas Fogg (the fat one)

When I was staging *Parade* at the Châtelet in 1917, I complained of a lack of light. "Monsieur Colombier," I said to the stage manager, "I'd like to recreate the lighting of the Vegetable Kingdom in *La Biche au Bois.*" "How old were you then, Monsieur Coc-

Around the World in Eighty Days

teau?" "Five." "The lighting was your own," he told
me. "In those days, the theater didn't have even a quar-
ter of the lighting capacity it has now."

Alas! I'll repeat it for you, the gold of the red
curtain and the blaze of footlights couldn't burn our
sceptical children's eyes.

Since I'm babbling, I remember a pretty, cynical
little girl on the Champs-Elysées. She scorned the pup-
pets, the merry-go-rounds and their brass rings, the
goats, the donuts, the barley sugar stands and the

pitcher of cocoa. She listened to me rapturize over *Around the World*. She smiled, shrugged her shoulders, shook her braids. She knew the play and explained that Philéas Fogg was thin. I had had the misfortune of falling on an understudy, and as my Philéas Fogg had been fat, I tried to convince her that she had misseen the play, that she should see it again. She made fun of the snakes of Aouda's cave. She kept repeating: "It's a trick." That hurt me, and it still hurts when I hear ladies watching *Tarzan* speak of tricks, of Hollywood's fake lions. Certainly, ladies, the art is in the trick. The great chase scenes are an art and, all in all, it is harder to make a lion from a throw-rug than to make a throw-rug from a lion.

I went back to a recent revival of *Around the World*. The new material respects the original production. My neighbors looked at me askance. Because the falsetto voices off-stage (which reminded me of Pougaud's famous delivery), Passe-Partout falling thunderstruck by an opium pipe, the black cook, the telegraphed S.O.S., the white skin of the Sioux visible between their short jerseys and their red leather gloves, Philéas' saddlebag, the palm trees of the Grand Hotel of the Indies, the bursting boilers, the sinking steamer and the wreckage to which Juve and Fantômas would find themselves clinging, face to face, riding waves of green canvas lifted on the stagehands' backs—this collection of naive marvels had me swimming in tears. Do we know whence such tears rise and what draws them from us? One night a few years ago, at Offenbach's *La Belle Hélène*, a friend pointed out an old lady crying in the shadows of a neighboring box. It was Cosima Wagner. Switzerland! Triebschen! Paul Rée! Nietzsche's words:

Around the World in Eighty Days: *Aouda kidnapped*

"We will go to see them dancing the cancan in Paris," the joyful youth, the arguments, the brawls . . . Cosima Wagner might perhaps have borne the *Ride of the Valkyries* courageously. She was crying during the *Royal March*.

5

The smell of the circus.—The acrobats' net.—
Footit and Chocolat.—The toreadors.—The
aquatic pantomime.—The cakewalk.—The Elks.

At the corner of the Rue Moncey and the Rue Blanche, the Rue La Bruyère opens out onto the wall and the chestnut trees of the Hôtel Sipierre. My German fräulein knew the policeman at the cabstand; she would call to him, announcing the destination of our little walk. I was sure that the news elicited the policeman's amazement and envy, and I hastened on ahead of her with pride.

In the Faubourg Saint-Honoré, a pediment crowned the doors of the Nouveau Cirque. Footit and Chocolat straddled the pediment, in relief and in color like the archers of the Temple of Aeginus. I have already told you about the mysterious path that led me to the foot of the ticket booth. The judges tore our tickets in two, I closed my eyes . . . and inhaled the great, wonderful odor.

Childhood has its aromas. I can remember, among others, the glue from the pictures we cut up in the sickroom, the lindens of Maisons-Laffitte that went

38

mad at the approach of thunder, the delicious powder of spent firecrackers nailed to the frames harvested in the grass the day after fireworks, the arnica of bee stings, the mildewed paper of an old collection of *Revue des Deux Mondes,* the canopy of the omnibus that took the family to church, unharnessed in the cool coach-house piled high with a jumble of pickaxes, hoses, croquet and hoop-ball games. (My cousin Marianne had shut me in that omnibus and told me: "Listen, I know it all. There are grownups who go to bed in the middle of the day. The men are called 'playboys', the women are called 'tarts.' Uncle André is a playboy. If you tell anyone I'll beat you to death with a shovel.") I include the heady smells of the farmyard dungheap and the soil splattered with white droppings where the greengages split their heads open falling from the tree. And not to forget the smells of the geranium pots in the greenhouse and the birdbath with its dead frogs posing like tenors, hands across their hearts. Later, I was to know the smell of Marseille that gives one hope, of ambergris exuded by the skin that makes one blush, of crushed lily in alcoves and of opium that speaks of a China of courtesy and tortures. But none of those solemn odors can eclipse the smell of the circus, the smell of the Nouveau Cirque, that great, wonderful smell. Certainly, one knew it was made of horse manure, tumbling mats, stables, healthy sweat, but it also contained something indescribable, a compound beyond analysis, a mixture of anticipation and lightheartedness which grabbed you by the throat, which habit, in some way, raised above the show, and which stood in for the curtain. And the rich depth of the childhood dungheap helps me to see that the smell of the circus is a wispy,

Josephine me conduit au cirque

Josephine takes me to the circus

flying manure, a golden, powdered manure that rises
beneath the glass dome, hangs rainbows on the light
bulbs and glory on the acrobats' work, then settles back
down, powerfully helping the multicolored clowns to
bloom.

Escorted by the usherette and fräulein Joséphine, I
would scarcely have emerged from the little stairway at
the top of a hatchway, when that living powder drew

my gaze, ringing in a halo of apotheosis the equipment, the tents, and the orchestra suspended above the vast nave from where the performers sallied forth, drowned in laughter and the booming music of trombones, cornets, bass drums, and tabors. The acrobats and the clowns dominated my show. The program set them apart, in the manner of the buffoons who fill up the empty rings between numbers and help to roll up the carpet. And even more than the acrobats' actual performances, I preferred their bird-catchers' gestures, the way they rub the soles of their feet with resin, the garments they fling away with a shrug of their shoulders, the final salute of their family, the so-called "graceful" running entrance and hop! their stop, hands held high, expressing a smile from their tiptoes to the roots of their hair. The net is a no man's land between heaven and earth. For, no matter how slow motion might throttle the rhythm of life, the film-makers had yet to show that within even the most vulgar and aggressive of spectacles is an angel that bursts loose, a smoke that rises, a sweet chestnut that blooms at its tips.

The orchestra stopped dead. The crowd waited, mouths open, and a drum roll accompanied the acrobats' tumble. The acrobats were falling. They fell, killing themselves flaccidly and flaccidly rising and walking flaccidly in long strides, in the gait adopted after death. Released from the weight of blood, they trod through a nightmarish pulp, a pulp of languor similar to the phosphorescent mucous that clings to the nocturnal mesh of fishing nets.

One number we liked, apart from the clowns and acrobats, was that of the Mexican marksmen. The term

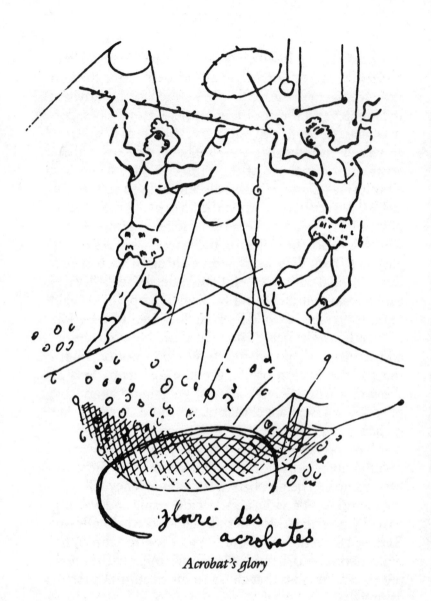

Gloire des
acrobates

Acrobat's glory

"cowboy" was unknown to us. Men and women, dressed in leather trousers and thongs, went about their lasso exercises that ended, at our house on Monday, in furniture reduced to splinters, tears, and the dark closet.

Footit and Chocolat came on after the intermission. A miniature pony galloped around the red velvet skirt of the ring, bearing the intermission sandwich board on its back. The audience got up, moved about, visited the wings. The stableboys, in their pale blue uniforms with brass buttons, disassembled the horizontal bars, hoisted the trapezes, put away the targets, the equipment, the tables used by the jugglers, the marksmen, and the conjurers. The girls selling peppermints, soft caramels and bitter drops chanted; the children did somersaults on the tumbling mats, the buffoons served lemonade, and the intermission came to an end, drawing me closer to the sinister retirement, to the end, to the exit where one grabs the wrong coat sleeve while turning a desperate eye toward the empty ring.

But we have not yet reached that point. Footit and Chocolat are about to take the stage. What am I saying? They would never have made the mistake of taking the stage and putting themselves on display in the music hall. They are about to take the ring. For taking the ring is not the same as taking the stage. That's like confusing a statue with a medallion, and I am astonished that the clowns of our day should accept parading their profile on a platform. It seems that the danger of not being funny, or just plain danger, can strike from any direction with the cunning of a bull, and compel the stars of the circus to make any number of Spanish about-faces. The obstacle of the footlights and the orchestra pit, the trap door in the wings, the dead end of the backdrop all

Footit and Chocolat

work against them. I have always preferred watching the three great modern acts of the circus: Rastelli, Barbette, Coléano. Of the three, death has taken the one who was the least interested in it. Death remains the partner of choice for the other two. Thus, Barbette continues to set it dubious traps, while Coléano dances with it on the wire, eye to eye. Yes, these balancing stars and famous clowns seemed to me to be wedded to the arena, to the circular rings surrounded by eyes (if only from the style of their costumes, which in themselves give them something in common with toreadors).

Footit had the sequins, the suppleness, the charm, the fame, and the glory of a toreador. He owed his fame and glory to children, the toughest audience in the world. In the corridors after *Parade,* I overheard a gentleman say: "If I had known it was so silly, I would have brought the kids." Those words of praise went straight to my heart. Footit bewitched children; his tour de force was that he also managed to please the grownups and return them to their childhood. Childhood can empathize perfectly with the nervous excitement of the clowns as they learn a new gag and decide to try it out on a friend, with the scolding tone of the head horseman, their refusals to work, the disobediences and the syntactical mistakes. Chocolat, a dopey negro in clinging knee breeches of black silk and a red tailcoat, was the fall guy for the rough tricks and cuffing.

With his fat, naked calves, his breeches with their pompons, his starched collars, his tow-blond wig, his cruel makeup, the grimace of his bloody lips, his pointy hat that gave off clouds of flour with every smack, his spangled corselets, his mad duchess's voice—in short, in his blend of baby, nurse, and British noblewoman (his hair bore the influence of Sarah Bernhardt and Queen Alexandra), Footit brought to the ring the atmosphere of a devil's nursery, in which children recognized their own cunning malice and to whose grandeur the grownups surrendered themselves.

The centerpiece of the program was the aquatic pantomime. How poignantly I recall the rising of the water. No filmmaker's special effects can take the place of that marvel: the tumbling mats removed, the green ring descends with a low rumble. Little plumes of water spring up between the floorboards. And now, as the ring becomes a pool, an entire set emerges. Waterlily leaves on which a dancer in tulle pirouettes, a transparent windmill whose rooms are peopled with shadows, horses and hunters plunging, Footit enticing a swimming calf's head to himself with oil and vinegar, and the China of *Papa Chrysanthemum,* a pantomime in which Chocolat returns from Paris in a beige bowler hat, singing the popular refrain: *"Tararaboumdihé, la grammair' ça m'fait suer!"*[1]

That was the Nouveau Cirque when we were seven. And five years later, in 1904, that same Nouveau Cirque was to be the scene of a historic theatrical event: the arrival of rhythm from America.

1903! The Minchin family taught us to dance. Madame looked like Dante and tapped out the bostons *Monte Cristo* and *April Smile;* Mademoiselle could lay claim to the poem, *The Daughter of Venus and Policinello,* and a pair of rather impressive winged dancing pumps had flown Mademoiselle's brother to the rich parquets of the Godillots (nicknamed "the Prince and the Princess") and of Madame Fenaille.

Suddenly, the cakewalk was breaking up and draining everything of color. Floodlights erupted from the flies at the Nouveau Cirque, silk banners in the American colors were flown on either side of every door, the first blacks (we had only known poor Chocolat) brought the solemn "Cake," a wave of elegance filled the tiers with women smothered in pearls and feathers, monocled men in crew cuts or with gleaming pates, the orchestra's brass and percussion sections attacked a foreign music whose rhythm evoked the marches that Sousa conducted and punctuated with cannon fire, the floodlights gathered like ballerinas on the hedge of blue horsemen, and the Elks made their entrance.

Never could the first jazz band at the Casino de Paris, accompanying the dances of Gaby Deslys and Pilcer, never could the negro from the Black Birds in his ocean-blue shirt, never could the roller-skate dancer, never could the Pancratium, never could any trendy, glittery show be compared to that apparition.

The floodlights do not illumine just anybody. They sometimes incinerate some poor devil just to highlight his solitude. Rare are the artists who glitter and sparkle beneath a shower of light. Mr. and Mrs. Elks shared that privilege with the diamonds and the stars. On its feet, the audience stamped, and in the center of that delirious hall, Mr. and Mrs. Elks danced. They danced, skinny, wiry, beribboned, glittering with stars and splashed in white light, hats cocked over eyes or ears, knees higher than their thrown-back faces, hands twirling flexible canes, tearing their movements from themselves and hammering at the artificial floor with the taps of their patent-leather shoes. They danced, they slid, they reared, they broke themselves in two, in three, in four, they drew themselves up, they bowed . . . And behind them, an entire city, all of Europe, started to dance. And, through their example, rhythm took over the new world and afterwards the new world of the old world, and the rhythm spread to the machines and from the machines back to men and it was to go on forever and the Elks are dead, dead are Chocolat and Footit, dead the Nouveau Cirque and, dead or alive, the procession goes on with its dance, led by the little canes and beribboned skeletons of the Elks.

6

*The young Carlier.—The Pôle Nord.—
Around the Concorde.—The Palais de
Glace.—The cocottes' hour.—Willy and
Colette.—Sem. Polaire.*

Once upon a time, two little girls from Montmartre dreamed about the Palais de Glace. They had read the ads on the back page of the newspaper, and those magic words—*Palais de Glace*—had fired their imaginations. A palace made entirely of mirrors, a sort of palace of mirages, that's what this temple of winter sports had become to them. One Sunday, our little *Montmartroises* broke open the piggybank, and, red with shame despite their daisy-covered straw hats and tarlatan dresses, had the courage to buy tickets at the booth and to cross the threshold. What a disaster! Rooted to the spot, they looked at one another, torn between tears and the hysterical laughter of young girls who are allowed to "go about unescorted." By that I mean that they were the first to make fun of their mistake. But the effect produced was far from reciprocal. If they weren't dazzled by the Palais de Glace, the Palais de Glace was dazzled by them, for these young gadabouts were none other than Madeleine Carlier[1] and her sister. (They did not yet bear that name.) In a world accustomed to characters who turn and turn like the sheet metal rabbit, palm tree, and Zouave[2] at the rifle range, you can imagine the dramatic impact of those newborn stars, those natural complexions, those four burning cheeks enlivened by the pink lights, the awkwardness, the contrast between the heat of the side-lines and the singular chill of the center.

When the little ones had regained the strength to pull themselves together, make their escape, and put an end to the escapade, it was with an escort of admirers, an ecstatic procession that was never to abandon them thereafter.

For me, too, the red diadem of glowing letters that crowns the Palais de Glace and which we can see nowadays from the *Figaro* had a powerful influence on my little person. I watched that circus from our children's corner, astride the wooden horses of the merry-go-round and held up by an ivy pole. I distorted it, magnified it, dramatized it at my leisure. But not in the sense of the little Carliers. I knew what to expect in there, and the prospect of skating lessons depoeticized my entrance in advance. A well-established dunce, the fear of any lesson withers my fantasy; and the magic of Christmas was destroyed for me by useful presents: rulers, pencil cases, satchels, metronomes . . . objects of study and disgust.

My brother Paul skated at the Pôle Nord. The Pôle Nord, on the Rue de Clichy (the present-day Apollo), was bigger and less expensive. I imagined it full of icebergs, polar bears, foundering brigs. The sign, conducive to dreaming, did not distract me, however, from

the Palais de Glace, because the neighborhood around
the Concorde, the green copper roof of the Madeleine, the desert island of Madame Hédiard, queen of
spices, distillations and disquieting fruits, the flower
market decked out in red silk awnings, the phantom
terrace of the Club where Swann and the Duc de Guermantes[3] had sat elbow-to-elbow, the Seine which Apol-
linaire described as flowing between books, the park
of pink chestnuts where the indiscrete iron benches
conceal the behavior of lovers, the Anatole Puppet
Theater and the solemn butterfly hunters of the Stamp
Exchange—the neighborhood had me by the skin of
my soul and, without my quite understanding why, it
still does.

My brother's teacher would order him to "stick to
it" and glide off toward some pretty clients. The
nickname "Stick-to-it" stuck to him and annoyed him,
leaving me with everything to fear from our first encounters on the ice.

In short, it was at the Champs-Elysées Palais de
Glace that my cousins, the Lecomtes, and I made our
humble debuts. I do not think the setting has changed
much. The enormous peppermint, covered in ice shav-
ings from the braking of virtuosi who speed, bent double, a cigarette at their back, and who suddenly spin
around in one motion, erect, lithe against the side wall,
to the little cries of some watchful lady; the orchestra
jangling its tambourines for *España,* or looping the
downstrokes and upstrokes of a slow waltz, the church-
like acoustics; the white powder silvering the orchestra
as the manure of the Nouveau Cirque, rising in a cloud
of dust, gilded the acrobat families—no, other than the

fashionable tunes, it seems to me that the azure plush of the draped mirrors, the rosettes and the canopies on the ledge, the light Moorish ironwork of the loggias, the little columns and the arcades, must be more or less the same.

Just as the Nouveau Cirque sparkled with water and changed its style at five o'clock, so the Palais de Glace, as if by magic, was emptied of schoolboys, cousins and families at five o'clock, giving way to the plumed ladies of the chic crowd. It was the hour of the great *cocottes,* who no longer exist, and the *demi-castors*—people who would be elegant *bourgeois* today

53

*j'ai vu, moi qui
vous parle ...*

I myself, with my own eyes ...

and whose dead ghosts make an enigma of Madeleine
Lely in *Amants,* and compel André Brulé to seek entirely new acting stratagems.

I myself, with my own eyes, saw Otero and Cava-
lieri lunching together at Armenonville. It was not a
meager affair. Suits of armor, escutcheons, iron yokes,

girdles, whalebone, piping, pauldrons, greaves, cuisses, gauntlets, corselets, pearl halters, feathered bucklers, satin, velvet and gem-studded shoulder belts, coats of mail—those knights bristling with tulle, rays of light, and eyelashes, those holy scarabs armed with asparagus tongs, those sable and ermine samurai, those cuirassiers of pleasure harnessed and caparisoned at dawn by stout maidservants, seemed, as they stiffly faced their host, to be able to pry from an oyster its pearl alone. Confronted with one of those beauties, one of our modern gigolos would turn tail and flee. A monocle, gaiters and white moustache, great age, and a great fortune allowed one to aspire to such encounters. The idea of undressing one of these ladies was a costly undertaking which it was best to arrange beforehand like a house-move, and in order to picture them in the center of a jumble of undergarments, mussed hair and scattered limbs, one must raise one's imagination to the level of a death-room scandal.

I should like to paint one of those tables with its snowy cloth, around which bustles a headwaiter with admiral's sideburns. The champagne bottle alone wears its napkin, tucked about its neck, in the French style, and everything else is correct, so correct that a vague smile is sufficient reward for Boldi, the red gypsy covered in the black signatures of ornamental braids on his jacket, when he has just played *Amoureuse,* his violin pressed against his whiskers.

Here at the Palais de Glace, braids adorn the olive-green tunics of instructors in black toques and shopgirl's ankle boots. They waltz. The *cocottes* call themselves Liane de this, Liane de that; all of the lianes drape themselves about the olive-green instructor.

Armenouville

Muffs at ease, they leap, swerve, bow, straighten, mimicking the noble curves of metro entrances, and, their
eyes lowered, they cross the rink. During the breaks,
their silver skates screwed to Louis XV heels, they limp
toward the washstands or perch dry-dock around the
tables.

Les tziganes

the gypsies

Willy, *Polaire, Toby, and Colette at the Palais de Glace*

At one of these tables gathered Willy, Colette,[4] and her bulldog. Willy, with his fat moustache and Tartarin-style imperial, his bright eye beneath a heavy lid, his oversize bow tie, his stovepipe hat mounted on a cardboard brim, his bishop's hands folded on the pommel of his walking stick. On our side, Colette. Not that sturdy Colette who offers us succulent salads of raw onions and does her shopping in sandals at Hediard's stall . . . A skinny, skinny Colette; a sort of little fox in a cyclist's outfit, a fox terrier in skirts, with a black patch over the eye tied back at the temple with a bow of red ribbon.

Sem[5] sketches. Armed with a Koh-I-Nor, the very devil's pencil, he slithers among the groups, taking up positions behind the goddesses of fashion and the dandies. Sem was a voracious insect, poorly shaven, wrinkled, gradually adopting his victims' tics as he hunted them down. His fingers, his round glasses, his pencil stub, his tracings on copying paper that he shuffled and superimposed, his wrinkles, his toupee, his umbrella, his dwarfish, stable-boy silhouette, seemed to shrivel, to converge on his will to bite, the entirety of his person knotted up like a handkerchief in order to prevent him from missing one single detail of the physiognomy under study.

In the changing room, we unscrewed our skates and our nannies berated us. We lingered and delayed our departure to the very limit of what was permissible. The idea was to cheat on the family hour and to witness, for one minute, the entrance of the *cocottes* and *artistes*.

And then emerged a creature whose name, even then, was a masterpiece in that precinct: Polaire! The flat head of a yellow snake, holding in delicate equilibrium the Portuguese oysters of her eyes, glinting with mother-of-pearl, salt, and fresh shadow, her features tied up tight and knotted to the nape of her neck by a black hair ribbon like a Percheron, her felt hat cocked above the fringe, a Lalique ring doubling as a belt, her foppish skirt revealing buttoned socks and boots cruelly bladed, the actress, as violent as an insult in Yiddish,

Polaire

held herself at the rink's edge, erect and stiff, posing as if in a hysterical fit.

A child's glance is quick to record. Later on, he develops the prints. I can see again, as if it were yesterday, that genie's silhouette perched on her skates, on her Javanese theatrical buskins. She dominates fashion. She baffles women. She excites men. Sem and Cappiello fight over her yellow profile . . .

7

Laughing at fashions may be hazardous to your health.—Mme. Letellier enters the Ritz.—Sem's hunt.—My mother's astrakhan.—Nature's false serenity.—Fashions fast-forwarded.—Lalique.—Dating plays.

I have imposed upon myself the delicate task of never desecrating the sepulchral depths and of not unwinding sacred wrappings. On the one hand, it is very limiting; on the other, it opens vast prospects for me, causing me to risk the picturesque and its injustices. For if we are tempted to portray the absurdity of fashions and the weaknesses of barren epochs, if it is easy to take advantage of the awkward moment that every acute form of lesser beauty must go through, then we mimic that mean-spiritedness that mocks higher beauty, that Parisian spirit, that hateful good taste desperately opposed to what Baudelaire calls the "most recent expression of beauty." Let us not forget that *Pelléas*,[1] the canvases of Renoir and Cézanne, flourished in the shadow of slow waltzes, of Delmet's romances, of the Salon, which every year returned the same fogbanks by Didier-Pouget, the same bathing beauties by Chabas, the cardinals at table teasing cats by X, Y, Z, the same white-shawled peasant women by Bail, standing over gleaming copper vats and enormous pickle jars in which tiny, curved windows are reflected, the same military allegories by Detaille, the same marble busts of ministers with their iron pince-nez.

Let us neither forget that the frivolous beauty of fashion and the search for it inspires or is inspired by solemn beauty, nor that, within it, one encounters prodigies that remain prodigious, provoking laughter only from such people who experience fashion with no understanding of its tragic laws. Fashion dies young, and it is that condemned look that gives it nobility. It cannot count on posthumous justice, on trials won by appeal, on regrets. It is at its very moment of expression that it must achieve its aim of persuasion. I have seen women entering a restaurant and glorified by the orchestra. This masterpiece of bearing and baubles sweeps away our hidden treasures, splashes them in a mud of light, relegates our worst impudences to the shadows.

Sem once told me that Madame Letellier, at the door of the Ritz, warned her escort of black-suited men not to be too astonished if they heard her flinging any old words left and right with a laugh, a sort of vocal babble similar to the sweeping brushstrokes of a scenery painter. This babble, which, from afar, sounded like an easy flow of joyous, witty conversation, served to overcome her stage fright, made her entrance easier, allowed her to "take it in stride." Sem added: "My job exhausts me. What can you do? Women achieve miracles of nervous tension. They can *hold* for hours and hours. If I want to be there when they *let go* and reveal

Le concours Hippique

At the races

their true faces, I have to stalk them until four or five in the morning."

Such a fierce statement gives pause. Tempting, certainly, is the moment when the miracles of fashion give way to others and unmask their absurdities. But such absurdity may only be short-lived. With a little patience, a mind that loves to love and despises the easy brio of insult can expect to be surprised. The woman who gives in, who *lets go*, who rejects the grimaces of

struggle, will become beautiful in her old age, and the old fashions will rise to that serene position where they twinkle like stars, where the eye can contemplate them beyond the workings of the world.

Certainly, the hieratic thistles of embossed leather, the irises of the bitter pyrogravure of our childhood, have gone to join Madeleine Lemaire's basket dripping with raspberries, the peonies which my sister Marthe painted in her watercolor class while sucking on her brush and reciting tirades from *Cyrano de Bergerac*. . . .

It would be only too easy to remind you of Helleu's dry-point etching that decorated young girls' rooms furnished in white lacquer: a lady arched against her parasol in the manner of a de Maupassant heroine against her handrail (a seagull on her hat, seagulls on the waves, seagulls everywhere); and of the Napoleon II hat of black cloth with high collar trimmed in silver and the bolero of cold astrakhan, with its ringlets like those of a faithful poodle, in which I buried my nose to inhale the perfumed moisture my mother brought back from her morning excursions.

Mountains breathe, move, slide one under another, climb, interpenetrate one another, and the secular languor of their rhythm escapes us, offering a static display. The film-maker has revealed to us the gesticulations of plants, and that a simple difference in tempo between the vegetable and animal kingdoms had made us believe in nature's serenity. A reappraisal is necessary—we have been way off the mark, ever since those marvelous, fast-motion films divulged the secrets of a plucked rose, the birth of a string bean, a crocus exploding.

We should film the slow succession of periods and fashions in the same way. It would be truly gripping to see, at high speed, dresses growing longer, shorter, and longer again; sleeves inflating, deflating, and reflating; hats plunging and rearing, peaking and flattening, sprouting feathers and moulting; chests swelling and

The astrakhan

shrinking, enticing and shaming; waists rising and falling between breast and knee; the surge of hips and
rumps; tummies advancing and retreating; underwear
clinging and foaming; petticoats disappearing and re-
appearing; cheeks hollowing and filling out, and paling, and reddening, and paling again; hair lengthening,
vanishing, growing back, tightening and frothing out,
and fluffing, and standing on end, and twisting and
untwisting, and bristling with combs and pins, then
dropping them and picking them up again; shoes hid-
ing or revealing the toes; braids knotting themselves in
itchy wool, and silk giving way to wool, and wool
giving way to silk, and muslin floating, and velvet
weighing down, and sequins glittering, and satins snap-
ping, and furs sliding onto dresses and around necks,
and rising, and falling, and trimming, and balling up
with the mad excitability of the animals from which
they were stripped.

Thus would we see the frivolous accessories of the
period in which our youth matured live an intense life,
never settle in an unbecoming position and provide us
with the superb, teeming spectacle of a veritable Me-
dusa's head, which would tell us more about a style than
any subway arch or Lalique pendant.

For lack of better, and since such an experiment
remains, alas, in the realm of fantasy, I advise you to go
see Lalique's jewels whenever they are exhibited.
Roosters holding amethysts in their beaks, tangles of
cornflowers, intertwining snakes, enamel and gems, an
astonishing and ingenious flora and fauna. You become
a little ashamed of the sobriety of invisible settings. A
goldsmith signs his era by tracing the inimitable paraph
of bank notes. (Shall I disclose that Paul Iribe is at the

Billiards

heart of this nest of vipers? As a young draughtsman with Lalique, he copied for his boss the snakes he carried in his sleeves and pockets.)

Another wonder is a hairdo of Sarah Bernhardt's —metal and turquoise flowers—unveiled by Sacha Guitry in the cloakroom of the Théâtre de la Madeleine, near Little Titch's enormous miniature shoes.

This in itself is enough to make us avoid laughing at art nouveau and to cautiously examine our disgust for the reigning fashion.

All plays mysteriously retain the stamp of linguistic habits specific to the brief period in which they were written and performed. The "Mademoiselles" in *La Voix Humaine* have begun, on the stage of the Français, to take on the air of the "Madame" in Racine's tragedies. I accept that and would not replace the operator exchange with an automatic telephone. For that matter, the imbroglios engendered by the telephone system of that day could no longer take place today.

If a revived play is only five years old, I believe that the actors should be required to stick to the fashions prevalent at its creation. If the play endures, those fashions become the costume,* and the playwright wins the game.

* One of the costume designer's tasks is to remove the absurdities from yesterday's clothing and to highlight its charm. Make no mistake, even a singer wearing period dresses must submit them to alteration. There are Carmens and Manons of 1900, 1929, 1935. Why not a 1935 version of 1930? Laughter would no longer be feared, and the eye would take pleasure in that indispensable difference, the disparity between the audience and the stage.

8

Booby prize.—My family tries everything.—
The real Cité Monthiers.—The schoolboy
Dargelos.—The marble fist.

In these superficial recollections, I find it impossible to pass over high school in silence—to my great shame. For I was the stereotype of the bad pupil, the pupil incapable of learning and retaining anything. My prizes for gymnastics, German, and drawing put an extraordinary slant on my misconduct, framing it, so to speak, in gold. If I close my eyes, my memories of high school are worthless and sinister: guillotine awakenings, tears, soiled notebooks, books thrown open in haste, ink stains, raps on the knuckles from the ruler, screeching chalk, Sunday detentions, empty classrooms stinking of gas, little punishment tables at which I copied out a thousand times "eight plus eight does not equal fourteen," in a handwriting more wavering than the serrations of a fish knife, suburbs, dismal departures and returns, autumn trains where the big kids tied us up with string and threw us into the luggage racks. I could recall other tortures: dormitories at dawn, mortal anxieties of being called on, attempts to copy from a neigh-

70

bor protected behind a rampart of dictionaries, a flood of threats, the discovery of compromising caricatures, cold sweats right up to the bell that elicited a joyful ruckus and unknotted my heart. The Petit Condorcet, the Grand Condorcet, Fénelon, home tutors! But what is to be done when the mind goes blank, when the child, earmarked for secret tasks and trying to sleep the sleep of a somnambulist, is rudely awakened at the very edge of a daydream by well-meaning assassins?

My true memories of high school begin where the books close. The playground is still under the influence of the cold shadows, too near the blackboard's chopping blade. Games and scuffles, pranks, truancy on the Rue Blanche and the Passage du Havre—these are the dunce's recollections that populate my memory of being a bad pupil and a freed man.

Crommelinck[1] wrote a play based on my *Les Enfants Terribles*. This unpublished play was to have been produced at the Oeuvre. Now, the battlefield of my childhood, its court of miracles—especially when the snow idealized and made it a sealed wonderland—was the Cité Monthiers, where one enters the Théâtre de l'Oeuvre through a gate on the Rue Clichy and which our army of knights in woollen armor and satchel shields invaded on the run between four and five in the afternoon through the archway of a building on the Rue d'Amsterdam, directly across from which were the doors of the Petit Condorcet.

It would thus have been possible, as it once was at Maeterlinck's in Saint-Wandrille, to request the audience to leave the theater and to watch the snowball-fight prologue at the very scene of the crime.

I will not undertake another description of the

The real Cité Monthiers

Cité Monthiers snowbound or, to be precise, bound in that shimmering mud and grey snow that I strove to reproduce in my film *Le Sang d'un Poète*[2] and which reminded lovers of the Russian cinema of its economical use of padding and bicarbonate of soda. It is true that the snow lay artless on the cornices, the gaslights, and the sheet-metal awnings of the townhouses that ring the tiny courtyard, a courtyard which our tendency to mythologize and to magnify that which is receding always makes me describe and depict as being much larger. The flickering gaslight added its own wicked touch. The shadowy corners grew deeper, the houses more fortified, and the soft, pale snow did the rest. And now that I'm trying to be fair, I find myself slipping, and would give anything to undertake some anecdote marginal to the first chapter of *Les Enfants Terribles*.

Actually, something like the story of the snowball did happen. A friend fell flat on the ground, and I imagine that the streams of blood that he spits up in my film—exaggerated by the same mechanism that drives painters continually to heighten Mount Golgotha and Christ's cross—should have been reduced to a very little amount flowing from a nostril: the trickle of blood that congeals on the nose of a dead hare. But it is indeed true that the fatal snowball was flung by the schoolboy Dargelos.

I must speak to you of the schoolboy Dargelos because he symbolizes the prestigious lout, just as Clinchard symbolized the wiz of composition within our little classrooms. One day we saw Clinchard's mother smack him in our mother's presence, under the cloakroom arch. Our souls swelled with hope when we learned that she had punished him *for being second*. He held first place, from then on, and was not to be shaken from it.

Dargelos, for his part, held from then on the last— the first place as the worthless pupil. But he held it with such strength, such daring, such assurance, that no one among us would have dreamed of wresting it from him or even coveting it. I might add that he was beautiful, with the beauty of an animal, a tree, or a river, with that insolent beauty accentuated by dirt, that seems to be unaware of itself, makes use of its every resource and needs only to show itself in order to persuade. This

The pupil Dargelos

sturdy, cunning, obvious beauty bewitched even those most likely to be insensitive to it: the principal, the vice-principal, the teachers, the tutors, the prefects, the concierge. Imagine the kind of chaos that a Dargelos, gang-leader, cock of the school, impunible lout, Dargelos of the midnight curls, the slanting eyes, the magnificent, scarred knees, could provoke in worms avid for love, ignorant of the enigma of the senses and the most vulnerable in the world to the terrible attacks waged by the supernatural sexuality of beauty upon all delicate souls.

I have always supposed that Dargelos was aware of his power and played on it. He was the vamp of the school. He dazzled us, crushed us, swamped us with his moral luxuriousness, and developed in us that noto-

Marbles

rious inferiority complex which is certainly overly dis-
cussed, but which exists and which, more than pride, is
the cause of many a heartache.

Dargelos held the lot of us in contempt. Receiving
a favor from him was at the heart of intrigues worthy of
the memorialists of Versailles.

I spoke of the "scene of the crime." Did a crime
take place? After *Les Enfants Terribles,* I heard and read

so often that the snowball thrown by Dargelos con-
cealed a rock, that I almost ended in believing it myself.
But the rock was unnecessary. I have always thought
that any mere contact with a Dargelos would suffice in
changing snow to marble, to harden it murderously,
and that, in his hands, it could become as dangerous as
the daggers of Spain. That snowball, the heart of a
scandal whose ramifications run throughout my book,
glows with phosphorescence. It hits Paul's chest like
the fist of a statue. The statue then repetrifies and no
one would dream of accusing it. Dargelos wipes his
hands on his woollen cape, throws his scarf over his
shoulder, dismisses his general staff, sticks his tongue
out a bit, winks, picks up his black leather "briefcase,"
and makes off down the Rue d'Amsterdam, abandon-
ing his victim.

    If I insist on this, it is because the episode sheds a
perfect light on the formations and deformations of
memory.

Now Dargelos has left my personal Olympus and, like the gypsy violinist who breaks away from the band to play among the tables, he serves up dreams to numerous unknown young readers. I have not changed his name. Dargelos was Dargelos. That name is a syllabus in arrogance. Where does he live? Does he live? Will he show up? Shall I see his ironical ghost appear, my book in hand?

I might perhaps be quite astonished to find a shy, humble, hard-working Dargelos, stripped of his fable and regretful, through me, of what he may at length have come to see as his faults, and have managed to overcome. He might perhaps ask me to bring back his power and the secrets of his prestige. I should prefer him to remain in the shadows where I have replaced him with his constellation, to remain for me the archetype of all that cannot be learned, taught, judged, punished, of all that singles out a being, the primal symbol of the savage forces within us, which the social machine tries to kill, and which, beyond good and evil, guide the individuals whose example consoles us for being alive.

Santos . Dumont

Jean

9

Great scandals in a semi-trance.—Loïe Fuller.—The woman of 1900.—The Eldorado.—Stage box no. 2.—Dranem. —Mistinquett.

It is in a semi-trance that childhood goes through events and settings. My German nanny, Joséphine, used to hold me on her knee and I would curl up under her napkin, digesting my soup. Fraülein Joséphine ate, and how sweet it was to follow that dinner, under the tablecloth, in the semi-trance of childhood. The sound of jaws and stomach, bits of bread falling, the soul-wrenching sighs uttered by governesses *crushed by responsibility*—the whole drama of a servant's dinner, complete with eyes and pinkies raised to the ceiling, came to me muffled by the linen and the borderland of a dream.

Linens and shawls and travelling rugs and sunbonnets. Streets crossed to visit a neighbor's magic lantern, the Saint-Germain forest at night, other nights of steamboats and Swiss funiculars, lakes shimmering far away, far below—far above, walls of ice that breathe, waterfalls that boom, hotels that smell of floorboards, customs checks, and the strange music made by the roof and wheels of the carriage. The way childhood goes through the great world in the arms of mothers and fantasy, thus would I later reinvent events in my own fashion.

Santos-Dumont[1] maneuvers his propeller; from a little straw gondola beneath a flying cigar, he waves an American flag. Sem sketches the aeronaut in full flight, his toothbrush moustache, his hollow cheeks, his soft collar and bow tie.

Between two policemen, her gimlet eyes shaded by an otter cap, Madame Humbert exploits the Crawford fortune, slays the ministers and entertains the crowd. The Charity Bazaar! Streets criss-crossed with moans, a funereal carnival of red wagons going all out, red ladders, red glows and men in golden helmets like allegories, sparks raining, soot turning into crepe and covering all the noble families of France. The luck of having been too young to understand the Dreyfus[2] Affair. The "yids," Forain[3] and Caran d'Ache's[4] paper, *PSST,* the anti-Dreyfusards of Maisons-Laffitte who stalk the ivy, wisteria, and honeysuckle hedges after supper, trying to sneak up on the Dreyfusards' deliberations. *L'Assiette au Beurre,*[5] where Caran d'Ache's pen has immortalized Krüger's jaw-line beard. The Adelsward-Fersen Affair[6] . . . Schoolboys recruited after school to take part in black masses, crowned with roses. The trial of the princes in Germany and the newspapers hidden away and the conversations cut short when one enters the room. The Tzar and Tzarina's visit, the Alexandra Bridge, the postilioned carriage behind the theatrical trot of Montjarret, Félix Faure's[7] groom, the Russian anthem that burns like Moscow, Edmond Rostand's[8] poem "Oh! Oh! It's an empress!" recited at Compiègne by Madame Bartet[9] dressed as a nymph and parodied by Ève Lavallière. The World Fair that leaves me with a memory more vague than any theatrical memory preceding it. Of that chaotic, dusty fair, I retain only one living, blazing image: Mrs. Loïe Fuller.*[10] What remains of the *bonhommes Guillaume,* of Cléo de Mérode in her golden breastplate, of the moving sidewalk, of the *maréoramas* and *stéréoramas,*[11] of the inverted castle and the luminous fountains? Is it possible, on the other hand, to forget that woman who discovered the dance of her age? A fat American, bespectacled and quite ugly, standing on a hanging platform, she manipulates waves of floating gauze with poles, and somber, active, invisible, like a hornet in a flower, churns about herself a protean orchid of light and material that swirls, rises, flares, roars, turns, floats, changes shape like clay in a potter's hands, twisted in the air under the emblem of the torch and headdress. Maxim's, the Grand Palais, Lalique[12] . . . certainly, they give you some idea of 1900, a glimpse of the design behind the firework display. Let us hail the dancer who set the fireworks off, the elemental force that shaped that ghost of an age in which woman (her undulating graces and undergarments) reigned to the point of usurping the place usually reserved for young men on the marble chariots of the Grand Palais.

The Parisian woman dominates the century, at the giant gateway to the Place de la Concorde, and everywhere—music, painting, poetry, theater, furniture design—the froth of her deep skirts will obfuscate all curves and figures until the day when African art,

* And Sada-Yacco.

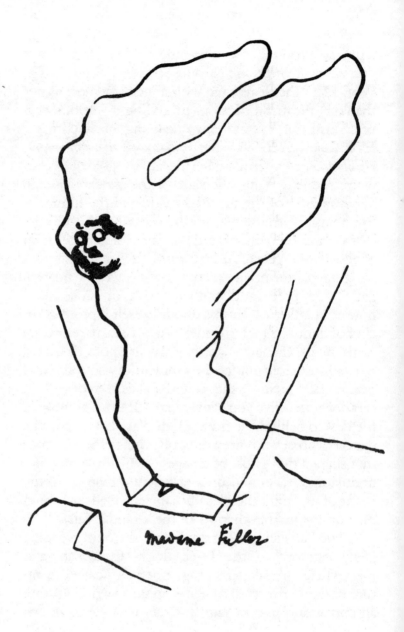

madame Fuller

sports, Picasso and Chanel sweep away that fog of chiffon and compel the victress either to return to her place in the kitchen or to submit to the rhythm of the stronger sex. It is true that the film-maker will quickly restore her privileges and allow her to reclaim her aggressive role as an *objet d'art*. I mean that she will draw her arguments against the thankless necessities of housekeeping from cinema, and in two magnificent incarnations—Greta Garbo and Marlene Dietrich—will find the embodiment of an ideal which consists in taking up her animal furs once again and brandishing the weaponry of sex-appeal against men.

Let us return to the time of my last article. Kicked out of the Grand Condorcet for misbehavior, I was preparing for my exams with Monsieur Dietz. After André Gide, I could but poorly describe this teacher who astonished us with the contrast of his protestantism and his odalisque poses. He stretched, flowed, knotted and unknotted himself, threw out an arm here, a leg there, observing us above his eyeglasses, shaking with ironical laughter.

Our escapades from the Condorcet on the Rue Caumartin brought us to the Looping the Loop (the old Pôle Nord building), where fashion dictated that we buckle ourselves into an anti-gravity chariot. There we met a little person who haunted our nights: Alice de Pibrac. She introduced us to one of her "girlfriends." This blond girlfriend claimed to have performed in a five-act play with Sarah Bernhardt. "Sarah," she told us between two loops, "wears a hump. At the end, she discards the hump and marries me." We thought she was lying. She wasn't lying. Her name was Lilian Greuze and the play was Zamacoïs's[13] *Les Bouffons*.

L'avant.scène
numéro 2.

Stage box no. 2.

Our love of the theater found ample sustenance on
the Rue Claude-Bernard, at Monsieur Dietz's. His son
played at the Comédie-Française under the pseudonym
Garry, and his nephew Pierre Laudenbach was getting
ready to become Pierre Fresnay. On Sundays and
Thursdays I ran off to join my accomplices, René
Rocher and Carlito Bouland (a friend who, from a
vague resemblance to Coquelin, drew the courage to

learn all the monologues in his repertory); we would pool our resources and rent, at moderate cost, stage box number two at the Eldorado. I might mention, too, that we brought along a basketful of violet bouquets with which to bombard the singers—a childish, awkward, cold, and wet bombardment that drew smiles and scoldings in equal measure. That stage box had considerable pretentions. It participated in the show in that it was partially wedged between the foot- and floodlights. I believe that its moderate cost stemmed from its inconveniently concealing the only corner of the stage visible behind the scrolls of the double basses and the skulls of the standing cellists. But the main thing was the proscenium, where the artists did their numbers. The hall swarmed behind a zone of luminous dust and backlighting. For us, it was limited to the pale blue plush of the rail of our box and to the conductor, Monsieur Dédé, a moustachioed and woolly-haired black man who wore specs and conducted in white gloves.

I pity modern youth, who have nothing to wait for but ghosts after a film.

Our band adored Mistinquett,[14] princess of the Eldo, and would wait for her at the stage door on the Faubourg Saint-Martin.

To tell the truth, our passions were circumscribed by the scale of our means. The top of the bill, Jeanne Reynette, was my particular delight. If high school had billed us just like a theater program, I would have had the standing of an American star. Alas! Just as I was at the bottom of my class, Reynette was at the top in the vocal number, and that peculiarity made us worthy of

Reynette—tops

one another. She wore her billowing skirt short, a baton, socks; her knees were less noble but just as knobbly as Dargelos's, and she had a sweetness that caused her to laugh at her own false notes. That laugh amused the audience and won her its sympathy. "What became of her?" you might ask. I can tell you. One day, the ex-

ambassador of Spain astonished me with a description of our stage box. He had these details from Reynette, who had become a wealthy benefactress of Montevideo.

I skirt my friends' companions—Angèle Moreau, an opulent tart in a red scarf, and Mary Hett, with her barbed eyebrows, the shadow of a moustache, and cheeky beauty spots—to arrive at the star of the place. Dranem had just sung: "*Ah! les p'tits pois, les p'tits pois, les p'tits pois*" and "*Pétronille, tu sens la menthe,*" an eye on his cheek and his hat over the eye. The orchestra charged into the maxixe and, under the hail of our bouquets, fist on hip, sombrero at the tilt, Spanish shawl wrapped about her high-society skirt, Mistinquett made her entrance. After the maxixe and the "*Femme torpille, pille, pille—qui se tortille, tille, tille,*" she left the stage under a renewed salvo of bouquets. Then would come the hysterics and the short-straws to determine which of us would pay her a visit, confronting the stage door manager at the end of a dark alley. The meetings with our "vocalists" took place at the Pschoor tavern. But no amorous reality could equal the minute's meeting, next to the doorman's stand, with our star, holding her flowered dressing gown across her chest and showing us the *bicycle* surprise—a makeup technique she still uses today, which consists of drawing the blue spokes of a wheel like the shadow of her lashes, between the arch of the brow and the edge of her eye.

Many years later, at the home of her son, my very dear friend Léopold, I was looking through the family album. At first one sees an almost ageless peasant woman, cradling a baby in her arms. "My mother," Léopold told me. Then, with every photo, the peasant woman grows younger, reaching her stride. The album moves counter to our middle-class albums, for the mother, ever younger, ever more elegant, perfects the famous face of Mistinquett, her great, joyful mouth, her eyes like those of an animal that cannot smile, her chestnut curls and her silken legs.

Mistinquett dances the maxixe

Mistinquett recently had her sister-in-law phone me to say she would be pleased if I would come to her review. She had reserved for me, at the Folies-Bergère, the stage box corresponding to stage box number two. It was thus from the perspective of my youth that I saw her emerge from a forest of ostrich feathers, perfectly unadorned in a tailored suit, without jewelry, approach the audience, overstepping the footlights and, there, sweeping her gaze across the rows, sing Villemetz's lyrics: "*Oui. C'est moi, me voilà, je m'ramène.*"[15]

There are several kinds of patriotism. I try to harden the outer skin that, in all of us, is sensitive to military marches, but why should I harden that deeper skin that would make Mistinquett's voice unbearable to me in exile and which makes me hear her as a Scot hears the bagpipes, a Spaniard the castanets, a Pole the piano—whether she is singing her plaints of a poor child, standing by a large dog in the manner of Velasquez's young nobleman, or whether she is explaining to the hall: "*On dit que j'ai la voix qui traine—Quand je chant' mes rengaines—c'est vrai.*"[16] Tears rise to my eyes when I hear that voice tuned long ago in the school of street cries and newspaper vendors, that voice made for wailing, that voice which is another kind of look from that face put together with hard knocks.

During the intermission, I brought one of the most beautiful young women of our day into her dressing room. Scarcely had the introductions been made and the young woman seated, than the following phenomenon occurred: beauty and youth were overshadowed by that woman who, in a moment, would return to the snowy set in a long, fiery gown, eclipsing the very young gigolos escorting her. "Come now," says one of my lady readers, "you speak of Mistinquett as if she were Duse.[17] What role can she play for you? What playwright can she serve? Who are her heroines?"—I do not know. She is her own incarnation. She expresses the very best of my town. She flatters the patriotism I am not ashamed of. Moreover, I respect that determination to shine, with that light so long in reaching mankind, the light of the very stars themselves.

10

Villefranche.—Hôtel Welcome.—Nice.—
Christian Bérard invents a mythology.—
The Captive.—The dead friend.—Madame X.
—The unknown style.—The goddesses'
revenge.

Tonight, I am writing my article in the Hôtel Welcome, in Villefranche-sur-Mer. This hotel is a wellspring of myths, a place which youth, infatuated with lyricism, should convert into an altar and cover with flowers. Poets of every sort and every language have lived here and, by a simple mingling of fluids, made this extraordinary little town—a precipitous jumble ending at the water's edge—a veritable Lourdes, a center of fables and fabrications. I will never forget Christian Bérard's contraposition, against the cubes, sheet metal, and crystal which threatened the world, of an aerial junk room whose origins one can detect in this archaic Nice, a fairytale city of carnivals, pageantry, battles of flowers, azure, plaster, and gold, a city one crosses in a dream and which astounds with its sordid ostentation, its red squares, its flower beds, its arches, its *trompe-l'oeil*, and its crowds perching on white chairs to ap-

92

plaud the procession of waves. Statues standing on one leg on roof corners, sun-shaded buggies, Chinese boutiques, English invalids, Russian families, fighting children, Pierrots dancing the farandole—I imagine that no Italian comic-opera set could more fittingly haunt the waking sleep of poets than this theater of illusions for which the little town of Villefranche serves as backstage. Yes, Villefranche, and the Hôtel Welcome whose pale blue rooms look out over the gulf, over the American or British navy, its banners, its Shakespearean fanfares, its jazz bands and hymns—there, Christian Bérard[1] instructed youth in wax faces, busts eavesdropping behind red drapes, women at sleepers' bedsides, a finger to their lips, barracks bakers in the full moon, kidnappers, little girls sticking out their tongues behind study room doors, holy cripples and other marvels that people your solitude in 1935 and would never have peopled it without our merry band and without the hotel with its gracious balconies of marble and iron.

What silence tonight! The town is quiet, the sea is quiet, the brightly shining boats are quiet (a little higher than the sea, it seems), the buoys are quiet, the lighthouse trails its megaphone across the cliffs, and a few crickets are mimicking the confabulation of stars. Four years' determination to live and solicit miracles, four long years, are piled up between the Villefranche where I am writing these lines and the Villefranche where we lived, where I wrote *Orphée* and the poems of *Opéra,* where, on my way home from Stravinsky's, I trod the Montboron road, my ears still dazzled by the golden, frizzy, curly ringlets of music of *Oedipus Rex.*

And tonight, before my open window, which frames the dialogue between the lighthouse and the red light on the breakwater, and the moon so crisp it would be naive to see it as anything but a ruin, and the dead water, and the boats hanging on the emptiness, I am thinking that I have sat myself down in order neither to describe nor to whimper, and that these articles belong to a far less recent past. Certainly, the past is only the future grown old, and the present a still youthful past. Past, present, future exist merely by a phenomenon of folding which allows us an outward and altogether fortuitous connection with eternity, whose inner design, similar to the paper lace cut by conjurer's scissors, must be dishearteningly monotonous. It remains true nonetheless that I have drawn up a program for myself and intend to stick to it: to tell, gradually and in any order, not of what might interest a few people, but of that which may very well interest a good many of them. Instead of writing my memoirs, I intend to solicit my memory, to stimulate it, wait for the result and, through a kind of guided freedom, a semi-trance, to see the formation of such-and-such face or such-and-such landscape, flowing from my pen like ectoplasm from the mouth of a medium. And tonight, as I force this strange clay to come down and take life, as I push it out through the mediation of these memories of Villefranche and of the guests who made it a dispensary of dreams, tonight as I wondered if I should ever be able to fulfill my undertaking to mail an article to the *Figaro,* I find an unexpected figure fleshing itself out, an exqui-

site enigma from my youth, a sphinx at the gate between childhood and adolescence, a gate which,
through a family blindness, sadly and all too often
leaves us only the memory of a padded entry into a
wicked place.

@

In September 1931, I had typhoid fever in
Toulon. Toulon, where I lived side-by-side with a monkey and an Annamite houseboy, is a moving city, the
real Toulon of *Consolata, Daughter of the Sun,* so long as
one remains in good health. It is less pleasant to fall
seriously ill there, when the houseboy loses his head,
the monkey wants to bite, and the hotels send you
packing. The clinic doctor, Jean Desbordes, and the
family of Edouard Bourdet,[2] were my guardian angels.
Denise and Edouard Bourdet came to see me every day
and I read *The Captive,* which I was only to see in
revival. Fever gives one second sight. Thanks to two
cues from the young woman—"She knows everything"
and "She never lies"—and to a sentence by Madame
Aiguines's husband, the figure of a person I knew, like
the Arlésienne[3] and certain Maeterlinck heroes, imperi-
ously stepped in for the character whom Bourdet leaves
in the shadows. It was rather like a head drawn with
invisible ink. Bring it in proximity to the heat and the
white sheet discloses its secret. And, in fact, that head,
and the supine woman who followed, emerged from
the shadows of my memory by the light of a winter's
fire, among the Chinese silks and furs.

I asked Bourdet if the model for the woman
who haunts the play with her absence was indeed

Madame X. It was she. As he was astonished that I should have known, at such a tender age, a woman who kept virtually no company, I described the circumstances of our first encounters, the friendship that ensued, and the impression which that friendship left with me forever.

◎

At Monsieur Dietz's, a very young pupil intrigued us all. His large head, that of a gentle ogre, exuded charm through a mouth that held countless teeth, and through unkempt locks and frightened eyes the color of purple ink. We sensed that he was very wealthy and all alone, despite the hurried doctors in their sable-lined coats and the tutor (almost a guardian) who made him jot down his dreams. He died of meningitis. They had moved him back home. His mother sent word for me to come see her, and we made an appointment for a Sunday, late in the afternoon.

◎

One must understand where I lived. I didn't know anything, and besides, the certain manner of decorating one's home that is commonplace today did not exist then.

I knew the Rue La Bruyère, its ivory and ebony tables, its dining rooms of chairs upholstered in chocolate-colored monograms on coffee-colored background, its extending table, the large drawing room dominated by the bronze *Florentine Singer,* the small drawing room with the swan lamp and the upright piano, my mother's room hung in floral chintz, our rooms furnished in white lacquer, Helleu's dry-point

etching, the *Bibliothèque Rose* and Jules Verne on the
shelf where we constructed May altars to Mary and the
Christmas crèche.

❦

  Thus, without any preparation, with no inkling
that there might exist other settings in other circles than
the plush of the notaries, stockbrokers, and admirals of
my family, I passed into the extraordinary apartment of
Madame X. who, as you may have guessed, was none
other than the mama of my dead friend. The parquet,
the white or black woollen shag rugs, the rice straw on
the unadorned walls, the Spanish furniture, the
eighteenth-century British colonial sofas, the red-
lacquer coffee tables, the anemones standing in a Chinese basin, the old silver of a kakemono, a marble bust
from Greece, sticks of temple incense smouldering in
the ash of a jade cup, screens from Coromandel, a
hammock hung between two walls by a little piece of
beige satin and adorned with dark purple Japanese
cushions, parchment lampshades, etc.—the whole style
which was to spread *ad taedium,* which you know by
heart—that woman invented it, brought it all together
for the first time.
  Reclined by a log fire, she watched me. I was
expecting our usual crepe- and tear-filled mourning.
She was smiling and wore one of those violet Chinese
cassocks that button at the shoulder. From the stiff
collar sprouted a thin neck, and this neck supported the
fragile head of the central figure in Carpeaux's[4] *La
Danse,* flecked alternately in silver or gold by her hair
and the flames. The face of a she-devil, a lady clown,
Bacchus, the face of a young woman or a young man,

the face of Barbette[5] as he grabs the trapeze and hurls himself—my friend's mother was toasting bread over the fire, at the tip of a little golden fork.

One can imagine the state I was in when I went home for supper. The family was at the table. I barely heard the reprimand. My ears rang. My heart beat. I looked on with a drunkard's eyes, and when I tried to say where I had been, to spit out my secret like an insult, I recognized my own impotence, my sacrilege, and, drowned in mocking laughter, I cried hot tears.

The Captive! Leaving Madame X's, I had passed a pretty young woman in the lobby, and was surprised by her colossal hands and feet, her preacher's hat and velvet tuxedo.

Only now can I decipher the enigma of that visit, of the gloom, of the haughty solitude, the sad smile, the forbidden sweetness of the son stricken by the furious goddesses of Lesbos, the barren island.

11

More on Villefranche.—A baron's misadventure.—Isadora Duncan.— Mounet-Sully.—Sarah Bernhardt.—De Max.—The ball at the Théâtre des Arts.— Sacred monsters.

More and more, Europe is becoming a chaotic factory of despair and death. In this enormous, desperate enterprise, there still remain a few places disguised, travestied, where merry hours can be spent.

Villefranche is one such place. It was once a royal landing stage. There, distant princesses were met by our ambassadors for marriages of state. The least of its little squares could serve as the set of a Goldoni[1] imbroglio, a Mozart comic opera, a cruel farce by Molière.

Shades of balustrades, palm trees, women doing their hair . . . On the ceilings of rooms overlooking the port, silken reflections ripple, an artificial marble of shimmering light.

Wedged between the ramparts of the Monte Carlo road and the Vauban fortress, Villefranche always displays the look of the eve of a holiday or the day after. Tonight, leaning against an archway in the covered city,

I close my eyes and remember laughter that will never be laughed again, or that, perhaps, may be laughed elsewhere, beyond the hearing of my generation.

Paris of 1912. Balls, balls, and more balls! The Babies' Ball at Madame Gillou's! Wintertime—it's freezing. Baron D., an old amateur actor in a sailor's suit from Old England—lace collar, naked legs, white socks, knickers, a hoop, beribboned straw hat—hurries along in his rented landau. Alas, at the corner of the Place de la Madeleine and the Boulevard Malesherbes, the horse slips and drops down dead. Baron D. must get out. A policeman reads the charges. The scene draws a crowd. Jibes and threats rain down. The policeman himself . . . "But officer, I was on my way to the Babies' Ball!"—"Quiet! We know that. Your address!" The unhappy codger rattles his hoop, stamps his feet, red with shame. He pulls his papers from a little pocket in his little knickers.

> January 1, 19 . . . The *Phare de Villefranche* relates: "Ball at the Hotel W . . . Among the lovely costumes, Monsieur de M . . . in a Phrygian cap of paper . . ." And, in the gossip column of the *Éclaireur de Nice:* "Flower festival. Very noticeable in his governess-cart, our president of the pigeon shoot and the fencing society. Iris wheels, wallflower whip."

This ingenuous press release sums up the Nice that stretches from Marie Bashkirtseff to Isadora Duncan, the Nice where people wearing dominoes, masked in metal mesh, pelt each other with plaster marbles.

Isadora! Let my reverie linger awhile on her, an admirable woman, worthy of those ages and those towns that disdain the rules of good taste, that jostle

Isadora in Nice

and bypass them. I should like to paraphrase Nietzsche and Wilde: *She lived the better part of her dance*. She cared little for details. She did not wink an artist's eye and did not retreat. It was a question of life as a whole, beyond the beautiful and the ugly, of seizing life and living it face-to-face, eye-to-eye. It was the Rodin school. Little she cares, our dancer, if her robe slips to reveal shapeless shapes, if her flesh trembles and the sweat flows. All of that is secondary to *élan*. Demanding children from men and getting them and raising them and losing them horribly in one blow of fierce misfortune, dancing at the Trocadéro to the Colonnus orchestra or to a phonograph on the esplanades of Athens and Moscow—this Jocasta died as she lived, the victim of a conspiracy between a racing car and a red scarf. A scarf that despised her, threatened her, warned her, and that she defied and insisted on wearing.

Our youth, mad for theater, was dominated by two great figures: Sarah Bernhardt and Edouard de Max.[2] It is Isadora Duncan who summons them within reach of my pen. What could they possibly have to do with convention, tact, poise, these princes of the unconventional, these tigers grooming themselves and yawning before the entire world, these forces of artifice at odds with that force of nature, the audience?

Mounet-Sully was in decline. That old, blind lion slumbered away in a corner of the menagerie. Occasionally, he would make a magisterial sweep of his paw: *Oedipus Rex*. Sarah and de Max often performed together, across from the Châtelet, where we saw *Michel Strogoff*[3] and *Les Pilules du Diable*.[4]

What ecstasy when the yellow curtain drew back at the end of the play, when the actress bowed, the claws of her left hand digging into her breast, her right hand at the end of a rigid arm leaning against the frame of the stage. Like some Venetian palace, she bent beneath the burden of necklaces and exhaustion, painted, gilded, tooled, shored-up, a dressed ship, amid applause from the gods. *La Sorcière! La Samaritaine! Phèdre! Andromaque!* Hermione is resting in her dressing room. Orestes goes mad. "For whom are—those snakes—that hiss—on your heads." De Max panted, shook the

Isadora débute

Jean ✿

Isadora's debut

103

Jean

Sarah

104

snakes off his own hair, waved Loïe Fuller's veils. A sort of poignant wail accompanied him, which for a long time we took for a backstage noise and which was actually the siren of the tourist boat at the Châtelet dock.

De Max was a brilliant tragedian. Like Madame Duncan and Bernhardt, he knew nothing of codes and formulas. He sought, he invented. He embarrassed. He raved. You felt somehow responsible for his mistakes. You didn't dare look at your neighbors; you were sweating buckets. Suddenly you were ashamed of your embarrassment. Cries of "shh!" stifled the last laugh. De Max, a fist clenched in rage, overcame the ridicule and trampled it down. His haughtiness bore it away and bore you with it, at full speed.

Can I ever forget his Nero in *Brittanicus?*—an operetta Nero in emerald monocle and train, who prevents you from picturing Nero in any other way.

René Rocher knew de Max. I think he actually went and rang at his door on Rue Caumartin, a stone's throw from our high school, across from the Passage du Havre where one could buy sneezing powder, itching powder, and stink bombs. De Max turned no one away. He accepted Rocher into his circle, and Rocher, drunk with pride, brought me along.

Like the ocean—whose gestures, roar, and seagreen tint he shared—de Max was "feared by kneeling mothers." (My own, trusting and perfect, was an exception.) "Your son knows de Max—he's lost!" That was the leitmotif, and it was falsehood itself. No black or

de Max

Jean

red masses. No traps set for young boys. Edouard de Max's intimacy evoked, rather, the familial interior of a gypsy caravan, and his alcove, that of Louis XIV. He received his courtesans, his favorite young men and women (a veritable harem of ravishing women).

I retain a photograph from my first visit, inscribed, "To your sixteenth year in flower, from my fortieth in tears," and the memory of a curious dedication from

Mounet-Sully that adorned the alcove, "To de Max, from his admirable admirer." De Max had that feline agelessness. That chieftain, that emir, that fat Siamese cat, that black panther, curled up in the half-light among the dirty cushions and furs, which our quick eye recognized as the costume of Hippolytus.

For the bric-a-brac of the Rue Caumartin was composed of theatrical accessories and furnishings. Heliogabalus's diadem served as chandelier. One had no choice but to sit on Nero's armchair or on the X of Ximenès.

A long time later, I came to know the Marquise Casati's bric-a-brac. I prefer her unicorn's horn, her stuffed boas, her bronze deer, her mechanical tigers, to the genteel audacity of fashion, the good taste that sets yesterday's bad taste on a pedestal and exudes no sense of enigma, of meaningfulness. A room takes the likeness of its inhabitant. It is the costume of the soul, a costume which our soul distorts and has soon imprinted with its own contours. Once donned by the soul, a room becomes the cast of our deepest habits. Order and disorder cannot be counterfeited.

Ah! How well can we picture your homes, Louisa Casati, who could never find an automobile high enough for your headdresses, Georgette Leblanc, who pedaled behind Maeterlinck in your Louis XV heels, Jane Catulle Mendès, who did your morning shopping in a dinner gown ... I love you and respect you, you excessive, marvelous women, you charming hurricanes, you precursors of the stars!

Disorder was de Max's style, his game, the whims of a warm, generous, oriental nature. In that ridiculed and feared apartment, which conformed to his soul, we were only given examples of nobility.

Marie, the old housekeeper with the grey locks of Guanhumara, opened the vestibule door. The guest crossed a series of rooms, which drew on the Fratellini's dressing room, a taxidermist's shop, a pharmacy from Coppélius or Faust. On an upright piano of pale green lacquer, carved with pink climbing roses, were piles of books by Verlaine, Baudelaire, Verhaeren, and Gide, in heavy missal bindings. One had to pick one's way around the twisted columns, the gothic coffers, the cathedral candles. Four steps led up to the mock-Pompeian bathroom; to the right, a glassed-in bay revealed a gloomy little Parisian garden. The dead snake of hose, the dead lawn, and the barrack walls. An arch separated the alcove from a writing table. De Max drew his ink from the mouth of a porcelain toad. He wrote in purple ink, in a tall, pointy handwriting, and blotted with powdered gold. A little bowl contained his fortune, which he would distribute to those poorer than himself.

When he went out, he sported a velvet suit with pearl-grey cording, stuck a grey pearl in his black satin tie, cocked the fat grey pearl of his derby over his left ear, gloved himself in pearl grey, powdered his grey double chin with pearl, moistened his dark-ringed eyes with saliva, and, in little patent-leather ankle boots with pearl-grey uppers, he went out, crossed the courtyard, climbed behind the windshield of his pearl-grey "electric," and there, stiff, offering the medals of his profiles to numismatists, drove quietly off to the Bois de Boulogne. He circled the lake, motionless, eyes heavenwards, a mole at the corner of a nostril, mouth bitter, and returned by the same route. At night he interpreted eight-act plays by Ferdinand Hérold and Paul Vérola: *Buddha, Ramses II*—what do I know?—every hero and every legend exciting his madness for costumes and poses.

Since this article begins with balls, I shall tell you about the scandal at the ball given by Robert d'Humières at the Théâtre des Arts, where he was manager. De Max, the most ingenuous man in the world, had dreamed up the idea of arriving with an escort: Rocher, Chiro Vesperto (a model), and myself. Our ingenuousness surpassed his. All we saw in his plan was an excuse for dressing up.

Picture, at the entrance on the Boulevard des Batignolles, under the dismayed gaze of Robert d'Humières, the pearl-grey electric brougham dumping de Max in an eagle helmet and veiled in an Arab veil, Rocher and Vesperto as Arcadian shepherds, and me as Heliogabalus, in russet curls, a crippling tiara, a train embroidered in pearl, rings on my toes, and painted nails.

It didn't take us long to realize our mistake. Robert d'Humieres had soon put us in a stage box, where everyone around us laughed in our faces. Sarah Bernhardt dispatched her attendant, Madame Seylor, to tell me: "If I were your mother, I'd send you to bed." I sniffed back my tears. The black smudges of mascara smeared my face and I was cooked. De Max realized his blunder. He took us away, removed our curls and our make-up, and dropped us at our respective homes.

This is not my only memory of a celebration in

L'avant scène
scandaleuse !

The scandalous stage box!

Mon dernier
souvenir de
Sarah B. dans Athalie

Jean

My last memory of Sarah B., in Athalie

which de Max had a hand. That great heart, among other crimes against taste, committed that of admiring my early poems and doing them service.

Out of his own pocket, he organized a sitting at the Théâtre Femina, devoted to my verses. The best-known actresses answered to his call. Laurent Tailhade combed his grey crest, similar to that of Canon Mugnier, screwed in his glass eye and monocle, and gave a preliminary lecture, a veritable massacre of the poets of the day. Only I was allowed to remain standing.

The fact remains nonetheless that my career dates from that reading, and that the efforts I later had to make to forget it are enough to make it unforgettable to me. But, in the final analysis, de Max had helped me. He saw further than my idiocies, sensed a hidden strength in me, forcing me to overcome myself and teaching me that greatness is ill-suited to delicate nuances.

Hail to Isadora Duncan! Hail to Mounet-Sully! Hail to Sarah Bernhardt! Hail to de Max! Giants, who should have as motto the response an Indian chief gave when he was reproached for eating a little too much at the White House table: "A little too much is just enough for me."

12

I wish I could make you hear them.—Catulle Mendès.—The Atreides' luncheon.—Scheherazade.—The death of Mendès.—Likeness to Heinrich Heine.

The blind man is a tragic character, the deaf man a comic one. You will not provoke laughter with a blind husband (in the true sense of the word), nor pathos with a deaf husband. And yet, the deaf are more enclosed, more driven from the world than the blind, and sadder. There are the merry blind, the blind who have fun; but the deaf carry an incurable melancholy. When you think about it, it is not difficult to step into the past through the eyes. Through the ears is another thing. We can pretty well imagine the scene of a supper given by Louis XIV; but the sound of voices, the manner of chatting, joking, laughing, escapes us. We picture an Athenian square on a holiday, and the ladies arriving at the theater as the cock crows at 6 A.M. for the premiere of *Antigone*. Impossible to summon up a sense of the clamor. The future will excavate the void and uncover fragments of fanfares, jabbering crowds, ranting orators. The silence of the past crushes us and the music of the Greeks remains an enigma.

If the line drawings that accompany this article surprise you, you should know that I make no use of contemporary caricatures—I draw from memory, I try to attune my writer's pen and my cartoonist's pen to the same rhythm. It is no easy job. And when I hesitate, when all that remains of the faces in question is a foggy resemblance, I strive for a line corresponding to my memory. The pen is truly impotent! A sketch is very little. I should like to convey to you the tone of those extinguished voices, smash that unbearable, echoing tomb, tear more than silhouettes from the ancient years, and through I don't know what kind of spell make you hear the ha-ha-ha that Catulle Mendès[1] appended to his least utterance, the muffled organ of Edmond Rostand, the laugh that Proust smeared across his face with his white-gloved hand and his beard.

I met Catulle Mendès not long before the reading organized at the Théâtre Femina by de Max (whom my uncle Raymond Lecomte, who scorned "mutts" and respected the proper use of the particle, insisted on calling "the actor Max"). He regarded de Max as the very height of insufferability and forced his family to share this verdict. I was therefore a secret admirer of Mendès, and dared not announce a piece of news that was sorely to test my nerves: after the Femina reading, Catulle Mendès had invited me to dine at his home on the Boulevard Malesherbes. Keeping the event to myself and waiting for the date almost made me sick. At last, the day to go to Mendès's house arrived. But first, I must try to describe for you the critic of the *Journal*,

Jean
A

Catulle
mendès

scourge of playwrights, playwright himself, and poet less read than illustrious.

I had occasion, during that long, heartless phase when youth seeks the *ne plus ultra* and turns on its master, to make fun of Catulle Mendès and to waste no love in depicting him. I regret it. May his ghost accept my apologies herewith. How could I better offer them, how could I pay him better tribute than in these souvenir portraits, in which I give total precedence to visual memories, purposely leaving aside those intimate recollections that assail us on our deathbeds.

Certainly, the palisade of Greta Garbo's eyelashes, the gowns worn by Marlene Dietrich on the Shanghai Express, and the young men's clothing adopted by these artists in civilian life, are all part of a new romanticism. Certainly, sacred monsters are not lacking in Hollywood. But sacred monsters in the flesh are hard to come by, and I believe that modern youth will find nothing to compare with the group of a Catulle Mendès and his wife, of an Ernest La Jeunesse,[2] a Jean de Bonnefon[3] with his head adorned by thousands of grey, goffered curls.

Catulle Mendès roaming the halls at intermission! I hardly dare undertake that description, and must first of all warn the public against the mistake of confusing the model with his caricature, the *black* of an etching with *blackness*. I should like to declare the admiring respect with which I approach a deceased figure who trailed behind him the august ruins of romanticism and the imperial robes of its gods.

Catulle Mendès was fat and walked lithely. He wriggled his hips and shoulders. A sort of aerostatic swell pushed him along blindly. The crowd, taken

Sarah dans le rôle
  de Cyrano
qu'elle joua pour la représentation
en l'honneur de Mendès

Sarah in the role of Cyrano de Bergerac, whom she played at the production in honor of Mendès

aback, stepped aside as he passed. He had something of the lion and the turbot in him. The fishlike cast of his cheeks, eyes, and little half-moon mouth seemed to be held in place by some jelly that kept him at a distance and placed some mysterious, transparent, wobbly density between him and the rest of the world. He had the reddish ringlets, curls, and whiskers of a lion, the prideful mane, and the tail in the form of a black coattail hanging below a putty-colored coatee, sloppily flapping loose on either side. A coatee, sporting the red stain of the Legion of Honor, that revealed the white, oversize bow tie, the heavy dickey spattered with coffee, the suit, the shirttail sticking out between the waistcoat and the many-pleated trousers draped over tiny, pointed ankle boots. His charming hand, pale and plump, held a Chaplin cane.

In such guise, opera hat tipped back, his eyes like a plaster bust's, curls across his high, narrow shoulders, elbows tucked in and cuffs sticking out from his sleeves, Catulle Mendès, the terrible depository of tomorrow's oracles, followed his belly, the light and magnificent figure of a prow cutting through the swell of theatergoers. He was escorted by Madame Mendès, a large woman painted like an idol, akin to some wondrous Japanese fish, behind the aquarium of her veils and followed by the foaming swirls of her pagoda sleeves and train.

De Max had dragged me over to the couple. Mendès and his wife had stopped at the center of the whirlpool. De Max introduced me, his famous voice slicing through those depths that made Mendès inaccessible to the timid, and it was then that Mendès, with that inimitable ha-ha-ha, said to me: "Young man, come share my omelette next Wednesday."

You can imagine how restless I was on Wednesday, and how early I was. I rang. A maid opened the door and asked what I wanted. More dead than alive, I whispered that I was there for luncheon, the master had invited me. The maid left me holding my hat and shoved me into a gloomy room. Little by little, objects emerged from the shadows. Very simple Chinese furnishings, a *bronze d'art* on the mantelpiece. Between the window and the fireplace, a marvel: *Banville* by Renoir.

I waited. And waited. At last, a door slammed. A subdued consultation . . . and the awful certainty that Mendès had come home and had forgotten me. It was too late to escape. Even after this I remained alone a long time. Suddenly, a door I had not been watching flew open and Mendès appeared. It was the strangest sort of apparition, for Mendès was wearing a mask, a veritable carnival mask with a lace beard. He apologized, admitted that he had forgotten me but that I should share his meal, and explained that he had fallen the day before on the Boulevard Malesherbes. The mask was holding a plaster on his nose.

We went to the dining room. In Paris and in Saint-Germain (his country home), Mendès adorned his dining rooms with an aviary. He doted on birds, collected them, and called them by name. The birds left their cage, flitted about the sideboards, cheeped, and pecked on the tablecloth.

The German pharmacist Schliemann paid for the privilege of penetrating the tombs of Mycenae and of seeing the Atreides, buried on their feet with their

golden masks. He had scarcely enough time to enjoy
this costly spectacle before the great corpses crumbled
into dust. Thus did I see, at the touch of this man who
opened up as the bottles were emptied, the great shades
of Baudelaire, Nerval, Rimbaud, Verlaine. Alas, like
the Atreides, they were now nothing but a golden

powder, a fog through which one had to guess at their shapes. It makes no difference—I'll never forget that luncheon, that omelette, the ha-ha-has of the master as he spoke, gesticulated, interpolated dates and anecdotes, and managed nevertheless to coax a procession of dead kings from his disorderly memory.

Thereafter, I took lunch every Saturday at Catulle Mendès's place in Saint-Germain. Same birds and same verbal resurrections. At four o'clock, Mendès got himself in gear, injected medication into his eyes and into his thighs through the fabric, roared while dousing himself with Pennès vinegar. Once on the move, he took the train and didn't stop until he reached the terrace of a boulevard café.

His death dismayed me. His maid announced it to me over the telephone. After a dinner with his friends the Oppenheims, where he had not drunk anything owing to some sort of wound to his pride, he returned home in an abnormal state and mistook the tunnel and its lights for the dark recesses of the station platform. He fell and the trains crushed him.

I stopped by the Hôtel Meurice to announce the tragedy to the Rostands. I had become very attached to Maurice, and he, François Bernouard and I had founded a review, *Schéhérazade,* the cover of which bears a naked sultana by Iribe and which was without question the first deluxe review devoted to poets. Maurice and I were the "boys" of the day. The era of the younger generation, inaugurated by Raymond Radiguet,[4] had not yet begun. We thought ourselves Byron and Shelley, and believed that, to be them, we need only speak of Oxford and ride down the Champs-Elysées in an open carriage under the April sunshine.

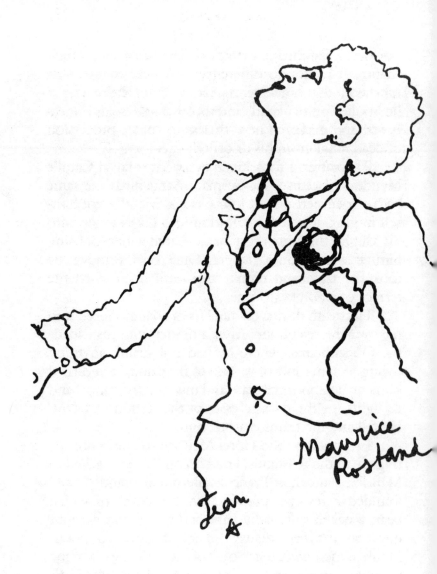

Maurice
Rostand

Jean

In Saint-Germain, a crowd had invaded the garden and lobby. Mendès lay in a little room devoted to the Larousse. Leon Dierx wept. A sheet covered the mutilated body and the candles shed light on a marvelously beautiful face. The face of a dead man recaptures its adolescent angularity. Napoleon's mask in Saint Helena displays the cheekbones and profile of Bonaparte. Mendès, dead, bore a likeness to Heinrich Heine, and I remembered a story that had once been told to me: in his youth, he had paid a visit to Madame Heine, and she fell in a dead faint because the likeness was so striking that she believed the invalid to have regained the use of his legs and risen.

13

Discovery of the Hôtel Biron.—Mendès and the moonlight.—Saving the park.—The "Friends of the Louvre."—Rainer Maria Rilke's lamp.

"Henceforth, Fantômas ..." "Retorted Fandor ..." "Juve was gripped with fear ..."

... The Fantômas style ... the bantering familiarity of Arsène Lupin ... the italicized wails of Rouletabille—that is how I should write about the entire period that I spent at the Hôtel Biron.

I had the good fortune of living in an enormous building on the Boulevard des Invalides, with five French doors looking onto a seventeen-acre park in the middle of Paris, at that pretentious age where nothing seems worthy of our genius, where no miracle can astound us, where we are sure that fate owes them to us and has uncommon episodes in store. I should say: the misfortune. For it is a shame that we are not favored with such extraordinary luck once we become capable of judging it, of appreciating its luxury.

Passing a day playing hooky from school on the

Rue de Varenne, I entered the huge courtyard of the building on the corner of that street and the Boulevard des Invalides, and asked the concierge if I might look around. I learned that the building was called the Hôtel Biron, that it had last housed the Sacré-Coeur convent, that since the "disestablishment" it was under the management of a liquidator of government property, that Rodin lived in the main wing, that the rest was for rent, and that if I should be kind enough to follow him, the concierge would show me around the empty spaces. If one of them should suit me, I need only make an offer to Monsieur Ménage, the liquidator. That very night I was in possession of the room I had specified (the nuns' old dance and music room). My yearly rent was the price of a month's rent for a room in a seedy hotel. A door, to which I held the gigantic key, opened onto an archway, and the archway onto the garden. Garden, park, vegetable patch, Eden—what do I know? I repeat, one needed the blasé eye of an adolescent not to be overwhelmed by it. Could it be that Paris was alive, kicking, bustling, working, driving, just beyond such a silence? For even if it only existed by contrast, the silence was no less imposing, smothering the ear to the eye's benefit, rising from the lawn and trees, extinguishing the city's uproar by force of that habit that makes silence the prerogative of a neglected park. It was, if you will, a *spectacle of silence,* a phenomenon arising from an old routine of sight almost always supplanting hearing. I mean that music distracts less from a show than the show hinders from hearing the music, and that the visual sensation of being a thousand miles from Paris, in the depths of the countryside, transported you instantaneously into the depths of silence.

To the right of the archway, through a little empty chapel decorated with lilies and doves, one entered the room with its many tall French doors. A stove, a piano, a sofa, an upholstered trunk, a few chairs and some kerosene lamps soon made the old classroom habitable and, from one day to the next, I was guiding my dumb-struck guests through a fairyland realm that bordered the gardens of the Rue Barbet-de-Jouy on the left and, to the right, the Boulevard des Invalides, all the way to the deconsecrated church where Count Osnovitchin held Russian festivals. I shall never forget Catulle Mendès, one summer's afternoon, thinking he was call-ing on some garret poet (after lunch on the Boulevard Malesherbes), and entering a setting more appropriate to a harlequinade. "Good God! Good God!" he kept saying, lashing my legs and furniture with his cane, passing a pianist's hands over his face and yellow curls, as, reciting hemistichs from one of his latest plays, he guided his belly with its shoddy waistcoat between the masonry and the gates. In her black velvet evening gown, Christiane Mancini, my companion at the time, had bought beer and sandwiches on the Rue de Bour-gogne. We had invited Mendès. The moonlight, as Madame de Sévigné says, more or less, had set out its linens, its statues, its penguins and its dead nuns. A fabulous pile of ruins and fragrant wild roses was heaped up in the middle of a sort of circle of sand and weeds. It was the only place that the brambles and branches had not invaded. The rest formed a little vir-gin forest, an impenetrable vegetable chaos. The mossy steps, the green-windowed facade, the sundial of the building (now the Rodin Museum), stood out amid the chaos. On the other hand, my French doors, difficult to open because of a thick carpet of forget-me-nots, gave onto a veritable tunnel of greenery, leading to the unknown.

If I am describing the chance that brought me the enjoyment of a realm that made us dream of the Hôtel Pimodan and ape Baudelaire's receptions, it is primarily because it seems to me to mark the last of the discoveries that Paris held back for seekers, like a private flea-market. Also, it is because fate had determined that this place of poetry should be saved by a poet. Indeed, one morning at the concierge's, I overheard the liquidator speak of subdividing the park and extending the Rue de Bourgogne all the way to the Hôtel Rohan. I roused the press. Hallais, Abel Bonnard, Chaumeix, Nolhac came to see me, learning at the same time that this treasure existed and was about to disappear. Their articles won the day. The ministers came in turn and were moved. In short, I saved the gardens of the Hôtel Biron and boast of it. I was less boastful at home about possessing a realm from a Perrault fairy tale, because that bachelor's flat would have brought down the maternal wrath. A stupid episode gave the game away. My mother was a member of the "Society of Friends of the Louvre." The Society decided to visit the Hôtel Biron and asked my mother to intercede with her son that the "Friends of the Louvre" might make use of his porch. My mother told the president that there must be some mistake, that her sons . . . , and so on. Letter followed letter. Interrogations . . . and the cat was out of the bag. My mother put a brave face on things and extended her graciousness to the extent of offering cakes and orangeade on my trunks, the day of the visit. But, alas, I had to renounce the luxury of a domicile other than my room on the courtyard, Rue Malakoff.

A long, long time afterwards, I was to learn whose lamp burned every night in a corner window. It was the lamp of Auguste Rodin's secretary, Monsieur Rilke. I thought I knew a lot and I was living in the crass ignorance of my pretentious youth. Success had sidetracked me, and I didn't know that there is a kind of success worse than failure, and a kind of failure worth any success in the world. And I didn't know, either, that the future friendship of R.M. Rilke would one day console me for having seen the light of his lamp without understanding that it beckoned me to come singe my wings on it.

14

The Rue de Bellechase.—Léon Daudet mimics Zola.—Reynaldo sings.—Jules Lemaitre.— Edmond Rostand's monocles.—The Empress Eugénie.—Audience with ghosts.

I owe many treasures to Lucien Daudet.[1] Other than that of his friendship and of my having found a second family in his family, it was through him that I knew the Empress Eugénie,[2] Jules Lemaitre, and Marcel Proust.

It was at a Sunday dinner that I met Jules Lemaitre.[3] Léon Daudet[4] had done an imitation of Zola for us, and, with his lisp, said the things Zola would have said regarding current politics and literature. One needn't have known Zola to appreciate the imitation and to feel its impact. Léon did not mimic, he resuscitated the man, and moved beyond farce to prodigy, to something that imposed itself, frightened, bewitched the entire table. From time to time, he scattered the ghosts with a robust laugh like a slap on the shoulder. Then, the table with its dishes began to revolve again, the lisping ghost was won over, returned, and regained its solidity.

After dinner, Reynaldo Hahn[5] went to the piano and sang Chabrier's *L'Ile Heureuse*. As at Madeleine Lemaire's, or in his room at the very mysterious Hôtel des Reservoirs in Versailles, Reynaldo sang, a cigarette at one corner of his mouth, his exquisite voice at the other, eyes heavenwards, the entire little French-style garden of his bluish cheeks turned towards the shadows, the rest of him, behind the piano, like a wheel coasting down a gentle, nocturnal slope.

In Touraine, at the Château de la Roche, Lucien became a flower and gardening expert. In Paris, on the Rue de Bellechasse, the flowers were paintings: Mme. Alphonse Daudet, by Renoir, evoking the heady embers of heliotrope; the Lucien by Besnard: a camelia, a gardenia, a corolla that is worn in the buttonhole, at the age of sanctioned frivolity, and the famous canvas by Carrière in which Alphonse Daudet seems to be a river god bearing away his daughter Edmée like Ophelia. Jules Lemaitre listened to Léon and Reynaldo. He laughed with a laugh that reddened his pate, swelled his veins, made his hands quiver as much as his voice, but he had not spoken a single word. It was at the moment of leave-taking, and almost in the entrance hall, that Léon later said, "What a marvelous ambassador Victor Hugo would have made!" Jules Lemaitre corrected, "I do not think he would have made a marvelous ambassador, but, on the other hand, he would most certainly have made an ambassador to marvel at." That answer sums up Lemaitre's mind. Such subtleties were lost on a foreign or inattentive ear. A directed mind. Directed toward what, you will ask me. Toward nothing; simply set, like a pearl.

Friendship alone determined the opinions of that

Reynaldo chante "l'île Heureus"

Reynaldo sings L'Île Heureuse

131

great skeptic, and his opinions were extreme through
the forcefulness of his heart. He made sprays of the
Action Française lilies and offered them to Léon and his
family, whom he adored and whose cause he blindly
espoused. His quarrel with Anatole France[6] dated from
the Dreyfus Affair. They were reconciled at a luncheon
at which I was present, at the home of Marie Scheikévitch. This reconciliation was held on the grounds of
skepticism. They moved comfortably about them and,
other than a few points regarding Joan of Arc, we were
offered the spectacle of a harmonious duet, of missal
illuminations, of Mandarin courtesies, between two
disciples of Voltaire divided by circumstances that in no
way breached their deep skepticism.

I never spent a Sunday morning at Villa Saïd. In
that gothic setting, I never saw France's astonishingly
long and crooked face, a face which, from his skullcap
to his goatee, was like a primitive sculpture carved from
some contorted medieval log or a Japanese ivory. On
Sunday mornings, I visited Jules Lemaitre. He did not
have Anatole France's entourage. He received me
alone. Pauline, his governess, ushered me into the library (his office), an old, glassed-in workshop which
took up almost all the floor space of his little house on
the Rue d'Artois. One descended a dozen steps and
found oneself surrounded by beams of shelves. Books!
Books! were what Jules Lemaitre radiated, and if Saint
Sebastian radiates all his arrows, it is proper that the
beams surrounding Lemaitre should have been library
shelves. For his pedagogue's soul was touching, young,
and fresh. One had to see him in Touraine, in his
steeply sloping garden on the Loire, happy to be back
in the open air. In Paris, on the Rue d'Artois, this wine

Jules Lemaître

grower gone astray, this countryman seduced into an urban affair, recalled his vines only in his wine-colored robe, the knotty vinestock of his silhouette, the peasantlike contrast of a pink complexion and tufted hair and a snow-white beard.

I was familiar with the yellow *salon* where Madame Muhlfeld played the chess game that consists of making a writer immortal, of pushing him from square to square until he arrives beneath the bicorn and cupola. In Jules Lemaitre's day, it was Madame de Loynes who played the game. Lemaitre was her victim and her triumph. With that Tourangeau de Tavers, she had won the game check and mate. In the place of honor above the mantelpiece, a portrait adorned with an artificial bouquet of Parma violets testified to her victory. I would occasionally stay for lunch. If it was sunny, we would take our meal on the garden side. I entertained Lemaitre, I soothed him. He called me Ariel.

A poet believes and wants to be believed. That skeptic could not like poets. He admired Heinrich Heine and those nimble sentences which, in Barre's rather thick, dry, swarthy style, play the part of angelica in gingerbread. He said of Mallarmé: "He is a rose thorned with morphine," and of Anna de Noailles: "She's a darky! She has Bohemian ancestors!" At Gougy's, he had bought eight volumes by Athénée (*Bouquet des Sophistes*) that were too rich for my purse. He then forced me to peruse them at his house. "I bequeathe them to you," he said. "Only, beware of Anna de Noailles! She covets them. Now, she's like one of those insects dragging along a twig bigger than itself. One day, you'll see her sneaking out of my house, dragging the eight volumes behind her." He would have feared me as a poet. He would have avoided or awoken me, the way wives avoid or awaken sleep-walkers. What he liked in me was my approach to poetry and its harmless manifestations. I think that poetry would have alienated him from me in the long run. Before his death, he read several paragraphs from *Le Potomak*.[7] "I don't understand one word," he exclaimed. "Not one single word. *But your prose has a rather Latin sound to it.*"

He often said: "I should like to write an article about you, to get back into journalism. Sadly, I cannot. We live in excessive times. We have lost the balance and sense of words. My warmest praises would seem cold. It would be thought that I don't appreciate you."

On July 14, we used to dine on the Place de la Bastille, at "Les Quatre Sergents de la Rochelle," the window opened on the street parties. There was the Comtesse de Noailles,[8] Madame Scheikévitch, Jules Lemaitre, and me. It was ritual, a doctrine.

Edmond Rostand joined our last meeting. Ever since *Cyrano de Bergerac,* an old misunderstanding had separated the play's author from the *Contemporains* critic. This meeting on July 14 was a friendly trap set by Anna de Noailles. It seems that Jules Lemaitre had been the only critic not to sound the trumpets of victory. *Cyrano,* he had considered, was merely the icing on *La Guirlande de Julie,* and had nothing new to say.

Our evening began marvelously. Rostand wanted to charm Lemaitre and charmed us. Suddenly, Rostand dropped his monocle, and it broke. Our waiter fell upon it and pocketed the pieces. The simpering cashier

requested one for herself. That was when Rostand drew
a second monocle from his pocket, which he gave her,
and a third, which he screwed into his eye.

Was Lemaitre irritated by this proliferation of
monocles? Was it the straw that broke the camel's back?
The fact remains that, after Rostand burned the table-
cloth with his cigarette and mischievously pretended to
be afraid and at a loss of what to do, Jules Lemaitre
broke his silence to say, in a dry voice: "It's very simple.
Autograph the hole."

The firecrackers, the shouting crowd, and Anna de
Noailles's spirit smoothed things out. But it was our
last supper at "Les Quatre Sergents de la Rochelle."

Lucien introduced me to the Empress Eugénie in
Cap Martin, where we were staying at the hotel with
our mothers. The Empress owned the Villa Cyrnos,
one of those steep gardens on the sea, between the
properties of Madame D., infested with croaking frogs,
and of Maria Star. On one side of the wall, Maria Star
(Madame S.'s pseudonym) strolled out with the cha-
subles, the chains, the rings, the pendants, the crozier,
and the corpulence of a Babylonian bishop; on the
other side of the wall lived the most touching, the most
out-of-place woman of the century.

Youth, entering, meets age, exiting, at the threshold. It is an interminable moment, a figure in a frightful
minuet, a night of the ages. As they touch, their hands
form an endless chain. I had to overcome my shyness
and laziness and allow Lucien, a veritable groomsman
in that little court of Cyrnos and Farnborough Hill, to
lead me to the Empress. The heat was stifling. The

cicadas sang like fever and quinine. The sea glimmered and licked its shores.

It is said that Tarquinius Superbus lashed at poppies and lopped off their heads. That is a symbol of activity. The Empress, for her part, hated flowers. She beat them down with her walking stick and swept them from her path. Thus did we cross an arid garden, all rock and cactus. A real Spanish garden, whose plants were stiffer, sharper, more bristling with needles than annunciation lilies.

I started to lose my composure, to fear the appearance that was imminent (the Empress was out for a stroll and we were going to meet her), to picture Winterhalter's[9] *Decameron*—the Empress, sitting amongst her ladies-in-waiting, infinitely less heartening than the Royal Grenadiers—when the meeting occurred, swiftly, unexpectedly, dark and small like an accident. And, as in an accident, I had every leisure to see the obstacle approaching in slow motion, to control my nerves, to feel no emotion, not to lose my head.

The Empress was emerging from a winding alley. Madame de Mora and Count Clary were accompanying her and appeared forthwith. She was climbing, dressed in a kind of cassock, wearing a priest's hat, leaning on a crutch, similar to some goat fairy. What first struck me was how little space she occupied, her size shrunken like a head mummified by the savages who killed her son, an inkstain in the bright sunshine. I realized that all that remained of the hot-air balloon was the burnt-out gas tank, the black heart of the poppy. What was lacking about this woman, in order for me to recognize her, was the crinoline, the pantalettes, the spencer, the follow-me-lads, the enormous, swaying straw hat, the crown of wildflowers, and the tiny, half-open Chantilly parasol.

The face is the same. It has kept its delicate, oval shape. It looks as if an unhappy young woman had buried her face in her hands for too long, and that the lines on her hands had finally left their print on it. The eyes have retained their sky-blue tint, but the gaze is diluted. A blue water looks you over. The blue, and the black pencil underlining it, reminds one of the tattooed eyes of young convict sailors become free old men. One is surprised to find in such old men the indelible signs of angered beauty.

The Empress stops: the blue water eyes me. Lucien introduces me. "I can no longer decorate poets," she says. "Here, I give you this," and in one motion she tears up a white sprig of daphne, hands it to me, watches me place it in my buttonhole, and continues on her way. "Come." I walk by her side. She questions me about dance. Isadora Duncan, the Ballet Russe. She tells me about the fireworks show in Cap d'Ail the night before. She stops and occasionally bursts into laughter. That voice, that broken laughter that hurls her into the past—where have I heard them before? It is a memory of the arenas—the laughter and cackle of the young Eugénia de Montijo, a laughter and cackle that must have frightened and fascinated the timid Napoleon III, the laughter and cackle of all the young Spanish ladies, stamping their goats' feet and tapping their fans in applause for a matador who has made a kill.

"Preceded by her retinue." That old jest wouldn't have much meaning in Cyrnos. The Empress exhausts her followers, trots along, is astonished by complaints of fatigue, offers to walk me all the way back.

When I take my leave and she invites me to return soon, I see that entire face, that whole thin form in mourning, lit up by a flash of youth, by that little lightning bolt of the lizard that puts life into ruins.

I saw the Empress again at the Hôtel Continental, where idiots were scolding her for staying across from the Tuileries. What remains of the past that could still affect this woman, several times dead? A habit. That of a neighborhood, stronger than any other.

The Continental preserves its style. Electricity is hidden beneath the lamps' gas globes. Lucien Daudet guides me through the lobbies, the Boulle furnishings, the velvet awnings. A door opens, dark brown with gold filigree. At the far end of an enormous room, the Empress sits, warming herself. She is flanked by the old Comtesse de Pourtalès and the old Duc de Montmorency, the Duke threadbare, cadaverous, covered in moss and lichens, his crushed hat beneath his arm, prodigious in his allure and elegance.

The Empress had learned that women were wearing colored wigs. She questions me. I reply that it is true, but that I rarely frequent the places where they are to be seen. The Comtesse de Pourtalès is revolted: "Colored wigs! The fools!" At this, the Empress swings around. "My dear, we had some of our own," she exclaims. And, since the old lady objects to the extent that she is able to contradict her sovereign, the Empress—implacable, hoarse, youthful—sets out to recapitulate the list of their follies. The crinoline inspired by Goya's Infantes, linen trousers that showed, tasseled boots, nothing is missing. And, as a finale: "*My dear*," she says, "you had a carriage with mirrored panels painted with roses." The Countess chokes: "Painted roses! Painted-with-roses!" The Empress has a fine time. She specifies. She insists. The Duke concurs entirely, recalling ancient scandals, ancient hysterics, ancient eccentricities. And I dare not breathe, dare not flinch, trembling for fear that with some awkward gesture I interrupt this astonishing scene, abruptly slam the Empress's drawer shut, or call forth the cock-crow and scatter the ghosts.

15

Simone and Trie-Château.—Anna de Noailles.—The Countess speaks.—Meeting with Francis Jammes.—Our arguments.—The river of the dead.

Lucien Daudet, Mauriac and I were a little group, and we rarely left each other. Particularly amusing to us were the readings held by the society poetesses. We never missed one. On Tuesdays, all these bacchantes met at the Duchesse de Rohan's, whose bizarre genius compelled a Max Jacob, a Claudel, a Proust, to learn certain of her verses by heart.

Dorchain had just published an article in *Annales* in which he spoke of these ladies. Except for the Comtesse de Noailles, he had said, they are amateurs. That article staggered them. At the center of a plumed flock, the Baronne de B., rolling her *r*'s, cried out: "Amateurs! Amateurs! *We who no longer count our feet on our fingers!*"

I was to meet Madame Simone[1] before the Comtesse de Noailles, and that was logical. No one could have been a better preparation for meeting the poet than the actress who served her and recited her poems.

Moreover, Simone shared with the Countess the luxury of speech: in a crisp, hot voice, rushing through her delivery or lingering over certain consonants, accurate as a sewing machine and solemn as an alto, the great actress of Bernstein's theater excelled at storytelling, depiction, at making you see what she had seen. Like all those who are able to see and who make their listeners believe they are embellishing, she possessed the genius of precision dear to those who have true imagination. You will hear it said that Madame de Noailles never listened to anyone. That's untrue. She and Simone listened wonderfully. They were divine at handling the royal civilities of listening. Forever ready to take up the cantilena and the fireworks, what was the point of getting prepared while one's partner is speaking? They knew how to be all ears—the Countess shammed a deaf woman's grimace, pushing back her black locks with a hand curled in a trumpet, Simone punctuating her silences with: "No? . . . Amazing! . . . You don't say?" which cut into your recital, encouraged it, and furnished evidence of a sustained attention.

And laughter! The fits! How we laughed together! At Trie-Château, the country home of the Casimir-Perriers, I remember one stay when the fits of laughter were prolonged and repeated, and split our sides, and gave us cramps, and forced us to rest on the stairs before going up to our rooms. Alain-Fournier[2] had just published *Le Grand Meaulnes*. Simone directed her myopic dreams.

. . . "Laughter that will never be laughed again" . . . It's torrid. The grass is buzzing. The stream flows. Flat on my stomach at the cool water's edge, whom do I see? Claude Casimir-Perier—dead. Alain-Fournier—

dead. Péguy[3]—dead. They are laughing; we are laughing. Simone talks, listens. A wretched cyclone is brewing.

Sometimes, after the fits of laughter, the windows grow pale; the twilight brings calm. Then Péguy reels off line after line of Hugo. He finishes and Simone begins. Her eyes lowered, hands clasped on her knees, she recites one of those vast poems that young university students know by heart: "You will be as dead as David, Alexander . . ."

Who could doubt that Meaulnes's malaise, that the acrobat-sleepwalker Franz de Galais, that the Eugènes of *Le Potomak,* sketched between J.-E. Blanche's[4] Offranville and Trie, are forecasts of the worst, warning us to take heed?

❧

Simone introduced me to Anna de Noailles in a car. She was leaving some lecture or other. At first sight, I must say, she flabbergasted me. Experienced at shining, at playing a role, at performing her famous exercises, and, thanks to the repute I brought with me through Simone's authority, the Countess, without the slightest preamble, put on a show for me to which her intimates were accustomed but which could make a bumpkin of any uninitiated spectator.

I must have looked like a frock-coated Fratellini in a shower of hats, in the middle of one of those scenes of carnage that leaves the ring strewn with old guitars, demolished furniture, soapsuds, saucepans, and smashed crockery.

I gradually got used to it. The little woman's beauty, the grace of her tone of voice in the service of an

Anna speaks

extraordinary descriptive wit, prevailed over all else, and I came to see, once and for all, that her sniffling, her turning, her crossed legs, her stops, her little open hands flung from her side as if from a slingshot, her movements littering the floor with veils, scarves, necklaces, Arabian chaplets, muffs, handkerchiefs, Tom Thumb umbrellas, belts, and double pins, all made up her staging, her technique and, in some way, the accessories of her number.

I must admit that, as soon as I sensed growing between us the kind of friendship that goes beyond the grave, I bolstered myself with every imaginable precaution. At the table, she required all assembled to listen and keep quiet. I have already quoted you Baudelaire's words: "Hugo plunges into one of those soliloquies that he calls a conversation." Even before she had sat down to dine, the Countess had got her grip on a conversation of that sort and did not let go. Did she drink? She held her glass in her right hand, while with her left she motioned not to be interrupted. And the guests obeyed. The mistresses of the house "presented her," repeating the leitmotif: "She's marvelous, that Anna! Marvelous!" The Countess went on. From her chambermaid to George Sand, from her valet to Shakespeare, she juggled, paced the tightrope, switched trapezes, performed card tricks. Let us confess—and it was this point that made me wary—she did cheat on occasion, lifting cardboard dumbbells, falling from the wire. Some failed to notice it, others snickered up their sleeves, others suffered. I was among the latter. I pitied her, watched her flounder, get into a muddle, suffer setbacks. Anything rather than return to silence! A sort of madness of the tongue, a verbal vertigo prevented her from realizing it. After several experiences (she occasionally succeeded in keeping her balance), I determined never to meet her in public and only to see her one-on-one.

And yet . . . and yet! Since I'm letting myself drift, and since I have proved my brotherly love by rejecting the hateful rule of censors which, when swung too hard, threaten to do a good deal of damage, I do recall a night of profound success. It was at the home of the Princesse de Polignac. I like the Princess, I like her way of fondly pulverizing the most irrevocable judgments, of accompanying her own judgments with a smile behind her veil and of bobbing her head like a young rogue elephant, I like her magnificent, sea-weathered, stony profile . . . and it was certainly to the fact that the evening ended at her house that we owed the good fortune of an Anna de Noailles in the full fruition of her talents.

The soirée was winding down. Across the pale Savonnerie carpet, the orchestra's stands and the audience's chairs were overturned in disorder. Suddenly, among this musical flotsam, I noticed the Comtesse de Noailles, seated and surrounded by a group of ladies. She was engaged in a singular exercise. Before it sings, the nightingale rehearses. It croaks and caws, it bellows and squeaks, and those unfamiliar with its methods marvel at the foot of its nocturnal tree. Thus did the Countess sing her prelude. I watched her from a distance. She sniffled, sneezed, burst into laughter, sighed heartrendingly, dropped her Turkish chaplets and scarves. Then she distended her throat, and then, her lips curling and uncurling at great speed, she began. What did she say? I don't recall. I know that she talked,

talked, talked, and that a crowd began to fill the large room, and that the young people sat on the floor and the old took the circle of armchairs. I know that the Princesses de Polignac and de Caraman-Chimay (her friend and sister), standing to the right and left, looked like the acolytes of some boxing ring in a dream. I know that the servants in short trousers gathered outside the half-opened doors. I know that through the June windows, as during a waltz in a Lubitch film or in the film of Liszt playing, the Countess's words bewitched the trees, the plants, the stars, that her words floated through the neighboring houses, suspending arguments and ornamenting dreams, and that all of it—from star to tree and from tree to the waiting limousine drivers—was whispering: "The Countess speaks . . . the Countess speaks . . . the Countess speaks . . ."

Poor, prideful thing! How she would have suffered in our hasty, disrespectful, inattentive age. Would Wilde be able to tell an apologue? I have my doubts. *"Once upon a time . . ."* Everyone turns away. Conversations resume. A syncopated din arises. Elbows nudge, legs kick, and Wilde stands, broken down, forlorn, pale, a purple carnation in his hand.

For that matter, I was told that, in her last months, the Countess fell victim to a mishap of that sort. At the F.M.'s, at the end of a tea table crowded with elegant young women, she had wanted to take the reins. A total loss. The young geese cut her short in the middle of a sentence, cackled, treated her neither better nor worse than a Monte Carlo gambler.

The Countess withered, grew pale, caved in, like

one of those Chinese nightingales that flatten themselves, wings akimbo, at the bottom of the cage, and die
in a fit of anger.

One other time, I saw the Countess in public and
in good form. She was to meet Francis Jammes, at the
home of Madame Alphonse Daudet on the Rue de
Bellechasse. Jammes was spending a week in Paris. He
wore a tobacco-colored suit, a red tie, and beige gaiters.
His beard stiff in the wind, his glasses crooked, cheeks
puffed out, escorted by young spiritualists, this superb
vermillion triton sailed from group to group, sounding
an astonishing nasal trumpet blast. The Countess came
in. Body drawn, head dressed in straw and red poppies,
she held out her hands and inspected Jammes. He took
her little hands, and leaned over the straw hat, repeating: "The great one! Here is the great one!"

Jammes's poems were read. He shivered like a
horse brushing off gadflies, his thigh trembled like an
examiner's, he waved a light-gloved foot like a hand,
one leg crossed over the other. The Countess whispered
to me: "Look at that! He's a veterinarian *who cured
someone!*" And a few days later (I had asked her about a
visit with Jammes): "We talked about the rain and the
sunshine. It wasn't much of a change from our books."

She lets these flashes of wit fly as if from a machine
gun. No one has better aim. So long as the audience
doesn't disturb her, doesn't make her morbidly giddy,
she hits the bull's eye with each one. The egg or the
eagle, she never misses. And, having shot down the
eagle, one might expect her to say, like the Austrian
archduke: "What, it only has one head?" For this
woman of instinct claims the erudition of a Goethe.

The electricity that leaks from her, astounding all, the lightning that caresses her, the waves she emits—she insists on taking them for intelligence. She'll have nothing to do with naive genius. She is revolted by Madame de Montebello's conclusion that "Anna sees Versailles with the eyes of Zamora." This revulsion would become the subject of long, intimate sessions "behind the cretonne"—the catch phrase consecrating our habit of avoiding one another outside and meeting only at her place, at Rue Scheffer, no. 40.

Ginet, the old servant, stinks up the cellar. He shoves me in a zigzag toward a padded door. This door opens on a small, silent room, a corner of the hallway that muffles all noises; books and cork on the walls, carpets stuffed with padding. The gloomy silence precedes a second padded door. That of the bedroom. I enter. Anna de Noailles receives, lying on a wide Louis XV bed. The room is the room of a young girl, circa 1900. The only difference is a photographic enlargement of a Minerva, forehead resting on her spear. Stiff, head bowed and helmeted, like the number seven, she meditates. But this pensive Minerva is not her patron saint. Rather, her patron saint would be the boisterous Pallas of the *Aeneid,* the grasshopper of the Acropolis, from where she descends via the Musurus. For surely it is not she, this Minerva, this little leaning column. It is not she whom Maurras kissed in the Parthenon. Maurras classes her, the young poet Countess, with those *grotesques,* those primitive ladies of the Acropolis who lounge on their tombs at their bearded husbands' sides, their smiling faces eaten away by probing eyes. What a contrast (the same as between the room and the

Minerva): these yellow ribbons, these laces, this cretonne, this furniture with its twisting legs, these knick-
knacks of every sort, and the lady of the house! Coiffed
with a crow's wing, a hairband, and a buckle (which she
nicknames her Vendôme column) spiraling down over
her shoulders, one would think that her wide pupils
were painted on a blindfold covering her eyes, and that
she raises her head to see beneath it. These false eyes,
these enormous eyes, trickle right and left across the
horizontal face. A powerful nose, a beak, deeply in-
dented nostrils for breathing in every odor in the world.
The graceful mouth, lips curled like a rose, reveals the

jaw of a carnivore. This frame, this animal skeleton, illustrate Lemaitre's witticism. What a charming insect! The microscope reveals an arsenal of sawteeth, pincers, and antennae.

Why did her death remind me of the sublime scorpion which, surrounded by flames, stabs itself to death?

Made for the grass and for "a rose tree to spring from her bones," made to be dead, she could not bear the red conflagration of the old world and its threatening flames. She was weary.

She loved purple, the symbol of power. This lover of Jaurès's hangs Mangin's sword at the foot of her bed.

It is fame she idolizes. Fame, her obsession! "You only admire failures!" she tells me. I try in vain to show her that France's privilege is precisely that of having secret glories, famous men unsuspected by the crowd. Rimbaud, hardly. Verlaine, just barely. Hugo! Fame is the number of one's squares, streets, avenues. His celebrity, Rome, and the number of His temples would be, according to the Countess, one proof of God's existence. "Anna," I tell her, "you want to be a bust in your own lifetime, but with legs to run around on!" She insults me, I answer in kind. Our arguments ended in my escape. I left the table. The Princesse de Polignac recalls coming after me and having found me at Anne-Jule's, the Countess's son, playing checkers. One night (the argument had arisen over my letter to Jacques Maritain), the Countess, brandishing a chair, chased me in her nightshirt as far as the landing. Doubled over, clinging to the handrail, she screamed: "*Anyway, it's simple. If God existed, I would have been the first to know about it!*"

Anna recites

Tender arguments, excuses for endless dialogues. More often than not, I was reproaching her for her formal conception of greatness.

She was upset with me for lacking *brio*. Love is without *brio*, I retorted. It cancels it out. One keeps repeating: "I love you." From the moment when I have chosen certain people, certain things, when I am ready to die for them, I lose the power of speech and its scales. The virtuoso does not serve music; he makes use of it. That's why it's better to hear him play mediocre pieces. He shines at it. Lacking love, you shine. Your love is immeasurable and nil. At least you haven't committed the crime of inventing yourself a love, like Barrès.[5] And the argument revived, better than ever. And I left. I went down the Rue Cortambert. Opposite the Hôtel Polignac, on the Avenue Henri-Martin, the asphalt, swollen by the sunshine, accumulates air, becomes a whistle, and makes little bird cries beneath your heels at night. That little thing, those cries from the sidewalk, was the last thing to awaken me, to distract me from my dreams. I continued the argument by myself. My heart raged, loved, adored . . . and, since time is man's invention, I found myself instantaneously, without having walked, at my door on the Rue d'Anjou.

At the window of the cretonne room, a tub of hyacinths was an obstacle which the Countess wouldn't jump. Forever supine, I believe that (except when she was inhaling the Amphion heliotrope bushes) she imagined the gardens, the corollas, the bumblebee (as bushy as the eyebrow of a Persian princess), through the hyacinth tub, through those scented sentinels, to be watching, erect, over her rare and meager rest. She slept badly, stuffed herself with sleeping pills, suffered, and spoke little of her suffering. She was thought to be a hypochondriac. Marcel Proust was treated like a hypochondriac. To say "I'm dying, I'm dying," instead of "I'm tired, I'm tired"—that is pure imagination.

I close my eyes. I try to see your smile again, Anna

Poets—*malades imaginaires*. And they die. What a surprise! How vulgar! They thought we were made of steel.

Anna saw a thousand doctors. Except as regards Madame Lobre, whom she loved and trusted, her doctors were pretexts for vocalization exercises. She didn't want her doctors to care for her. She wanted to care for her doctors.

She died. Life died. Dead is she of whom Barrès said: "She is the most sensitive point of the universe"— and "Her little body of a Spanish Christ." She wanted to be embalmed. I dared not see her embalmed. Embalmed, I picture her like Thaïs,[6] in the Guimet museum. Amid falling leaves, an explosion of old cigars, withered roses and bandages, Thaïs floats face up in the river of the dead. One morning at the Guimet museum, I saw a white priest on his knees before the glass. He wore the heart and cross of Father de Foucauld. It was Father Charles. He was praying. I had forgotten that the mummy was that of Saint Thaïs.

ⓐ

When I die, I will go to see Anna de Noailles. I will cross the lobby of clouds. I'll open the door and hear her argumentative voice: "My dear, you see, there's nothing, nothing afterwards. You remember . . . I told you so!" And to my eternal joy, it all begins again. The Countess speaks.

16

The scallop-shell pilgrim.—Crown of immortelles.—Gratitude to Gide.—Sacha Guitry.—The boxes flow.—Poiret.—Dancing on the volcano.

One must not begrudge those who recount their memories with a hasty pen and make mistakes. They write, not of what was, but of what is, of what remains of what they lived; and they work behind distorting fogs. Being offended by an imprecision would be like being upset by a souvenir portrait from a fairground because it shows you as a boxer, a driver, a toreador: "That's not him! That's not her!" Besides, the instinctive choice of setting says a lot about the sitter.

I might add that I live too far away to correct my proofs. Journalism hurries along, its pilgrim's staff adorned with scallop shells. It will be understood that it's not my fault if a comma is misplaced and changes the meaning of a sentence, if a singular becomes a plural. In the Villefranche sunshine, I watch for the mishaps and *it gives me a pain*. (Mme. de Sévigné wrote:

"I have a pain in my daughter.") I am counting on the reader's good will. His eye corrects for me.

History is made up of imprecisions. It resembles that death's-head by Holbein. Close up and straight on, its stains and smears are all distorted. One must stand back, at the proper angle, for the stains to gather themselves, to coordinate, and allow the death's head to be seen. The details are irrelevant. The masses, the volumes, the big picture of a man or an act, are all that count.

One must also be aware of the phenomenon of abstract perspective that magnifies events, places, and people as they recede from us. What they gain in lyricism, they lose in the contact of contours. The Golgotha of painters raises the cross, distances the Christ. Catherine Emmerich[1] brings them closer, reduces the cross and the Skull Mount to reasonable proportions, reminding us of what a nail piercing the flesh is all about.

It is thus, by a judicious dose of the vast and the small, that the memorialist achieves likeness. Why hark back to the storybook? It is hard to imagine the Queen of the Amazons writing: "Alexander's sweat did not smell of violets." The historian could well answer: "Perhaps your husband managed to avoid perspiring in your presence" or "you did not live together very long," and so on . . .

My work for the *Figaro* presented some serious pitfalls. I had to move from color to color, never allow myself to be tempted by the gentle blending of one thing into the next, by the rainbow of tones at the point where they meet on the necks of the pigeons and on the asparagus. I had to avoid the temptation to be moved,

to loiter, to complain, to boast, to open my heart. I had
to reflect like those mirrors that do not reflect, slip those
mirrors from my pocket and hastily replace them,
blindly take away the imprint the boxer leaves on the
canvas of the boxing ring, the reflection of a smile in a
looking-glass frame, trace the shadow of a profile on the
wall with a pencil.

And for what! Precision? Imprecision? Bees of Sol-
omon, how to discern you in our crowns of immortelles?

A gentleman whose stationery is engraved with
commonplaces—Legion of Honor, laurels, telephone,
telegraph—scolds me for littering my work with commonplaces. I would blush for shame if journalism
hadn't set me the example, and if the light style it
requires did not involve the use of clichés, some unmiti-
gated, others superb, solid on their pedestals, made of
pure marble, veritable masterpieces of the centuries.
Were they ever born? Do they spring fatherless from
excavated soil?

A farmer discovers the Venus de Milo's arms. To
whom do they belong? To the farmer or to the Venus
de Milo? They belong to myth. They encircle the neck
of poetry. They are white snakes, living their own lives.

How sweet it is to use "Besides . . . I might add . . .
I said . . . For that matter . . . In short," which embed
themselves as naturally as the last piece of the puzzle!

Forgive me, reader. Understand me. Help me.
Play with me. Don't just stand there at my table. It is
fitting that we write and read this punch-and-stencil
prose together.

It is to Gide that I owe these souvenir portraits, if indeed they deserve to live at all. Gide reproached me (in connection with a note in *Le Coq et l'Arlequin*[2] on early jazz) for never letting myself go, never using relaxation to my advantage. Writing with one's blood, shouting out one's love on a wall with chalk, requires breathing spells. I have pleaded too often against the sublime not to be suspicious of it.

Just as I owe these articles to Gide, I owe *Les Enfants Terribles* to Jacques Chardonne.[3] He scolded me: "You have 'masterpiece' block. A blank sheet of paper paralyzes you. Just begin with any old thing. Write 'One winter's night . . .' and go on from there . . ." (a sentence of that kind opens my film: "While in the distance boomed the cannons of Fontenoy, in a humble room, a young man . . ."—a sentence in which disciples of Freud found hidden meanings and which expresses nothing other than the courageous initiation of a work.) I wrote: "The Cité Monthiers is nestled between the Rue d'Amsterdam . . ." and the book that must have been waiting inside me slipped in behind, in one sitting.

And now I'm being smothered by all that I've suppressed. I am not speaking of the important things that had to be suppressed, but of silhouettes worthy of taking their places at the photographer's door.

Have I told you about nos. 8 and 10, Rue d'Anjou? About no. 8, where La Fayette died and where Edmond Sée[4] is living in Sacha Guitry's[5] apartment? Sacha was our immediate neighbor. I took the stairs four at a time. I blazed past the door on the second floor—the door of Madame de Guermantes, where I will soon show you Proust standing guard—I went from one archway to another and climbed Sacha's spiral staircase. At the top, a life-sized caricature of me indicated the doorbell to visitors. I knocked a pre-arranged number of times and delightedly entered his home, he who lightened the heavy city's load, who dispersed the miasma, who held the treasure of France's high spirits balanced on his nose, in the midst of the low spirits of ever-sulking Paris. Sacha was painting the L.S.K. poster. That clown and that checkerboard were to achieve a fame we could hardly have predicted. We lived, we were happy, merry, unscathed by calculation.

Sacha's only calculation was to write, in one night, standing at his desk, sparkling plays in which he did not make his entrance until the second act, and then only in a dressing gown. And so Charlotte Lysès left first, and we took our coffee without fuss.

Iribe, nicknamed Brother Iribus! Madeleine Carlier! Does Iribe recall our visit to the old Témoin, on the Place de la Bourse? I do not dare describe my clothing, my tie, my gaiters. I carried one of Madeleine's white spitzes under my arm. At Madame Lanvin's, she threw together tailored suits made from Indian shawls and ostrich-feather bonnets copied from engravings of Directoire fashions. A funny sort of couple, I assure you! I must admit that I have preserved my soul from those times and I am sometimes astonished at losing contact with other souls who were able to improve with age. As for Sacha and Iribe, we cannot meet without a tide of memories leaping to our tongues and hearts.

I have talked about eccentric apparel. At Tiarko

madeleine Carlier

Richepin's wedding, I was best man along with
Maurice Rostand and the Misses Luro, the bride's sister
and cousin. I wore a frock coat, a top hat, and a violet
carnation (*sic*). The caterers snickered as I passed, and
my mother, at the window on the Avenue Malakoff,
wept at my absurdity. Sacha (with whom I was not yet
chummy) appeared in the procession on the arm of
Cora Laparcerie, in a foot soldier's uniform—he was
doing a stint in the military. Sacha and Tiarko were
composing an operetta, *Tell Père, Tell Fils*. A tune from
the operetta, "*Je suis concierge du palais,*" slowed down
on the organ, served as the wedding march. The lyrics
silently asserted themselves, making the procession
shake with repressed laughter.

What gave me the ridiculous idea, one autumn evening several years later, to put on a fake Santa Claus beard, roam the halls of the Hôtel Biron, and at twilight to play the character of Rodin, whom Tiarko wished to meet? My behavior made him think at first that Rodin was senile. And as I called out: "Tiarko! Tiarko! It's me, Jean!" he thought Rodin had gone mad, and flew from my park as fast as his legs could carry him.

At Sacha's, near Honfleur, in the house made famous by *La Pèlerine Écossaise,*[6] a similar kind of prank almost went sour. We were mimicking, *grosso modo,* our dear doctor Mardrus and his wife. We had shown up unexpectedly. Now, Ajalbert feared and avoided the Mardruses. "Too late," cried Charlotte Lysès, "here they are!" And the misunderstanding was set in motion. The worse Sacha played his role, blackened with cork, the more I laughed beneath my veils, the more poor Ajalbert, blinded by embarrassment, believed us and considered himself ill-used.

I'd like to work in double time, to banter, to tell stories. But what is that dress Lysès is wearing in *Nono*? Those wide black-and-white stripes, that green turban, that Empire waist? A capital insignium has marked the city's whimsical soul: the insignium of Paul Poiret.

The stiffness of Polaire and the Lianas is already unwinding. Corsets are loosening. The gold of the theater boxes no longer frames *cocottes* in armor and dog collars. All those rigid lines are crumbling, the boxes flow, and we see the typical box of that transition period emerge. A side dish of meringues and ice cream: Edwards standing; springing from his soft shirt, an ectoplasm draws itself into a liquid mass, a female Eu

les loges coulent

The boxes drip

gène with splendid eyes, a poodle's hair, the mouth of a carp: Lanthelme.

The duchesses are ready for Paul Poiret[7] to dress them, undress them, put them in costume. Iribe's album disgusts mothers. It has not yet come to uncovering the stomach, walking like a crab and a praying mantis, a hand on the hip, the jaw cruel and haughty. It is a question of being the belly dancers, the silk and fur upholstery, the lampshades, the harem pillows of a

Poiret
approche en
silence

Poiret draws silently near

fashionable sultan. A pale sultan, a chestnut-bearded emir with prominent eyes, a comedian like Nero, turning women into odalisques, and himself capable of embodying countless types with the rags he gathers about him. Try to remember, Derain. On armistice night, Poiret disguised himself, metamorphosed, invented, mimed, aroused, so long and so well that at dawn we thought it was 11 P.M., like those travelers in a German ballad, victims of the nightingale.

And there we are. I should like to leave you quickly. I hate stations, trains that move off, unwinding the spool of one's heart.

Like the cedar in Jussieu's hat, Pepito and Manolo Martinez bring the tango in a gramophone box. From the Villa Montmorency (between Bergson and Gide), the tango was going to invade Europe. Couples intertwined, their shoulders still, perform the slow Argentine stroll. Fat gentlemen slid along with little steps, back and forth, facing their partners. From time to time they stopped, turned around, lifted a foot and inspected its sole as if they had stepped in some horror.

And here's the fox trot and the *très moutarde* and the elegant ladies with the aggressive elbows leaping about to *Sambre-et-Meuse*.

The earth trembles. More sensitive than the frivolous vermin who inhabit it, it senses, like a cow, the storm gathering in the east. Old and young rub against one another and jump. The earth trembles and shakes them all.

From a distance, we are always surprised that art should superimpose itself on catastrophes that would seem to destroy it. On the contrary. The crowd directs its foolishness elsewhere and leaves the field free.

The tango!

By its sacrifice, dead youth commands the respect of the old for surviving youth, and never does art evolve faster.

One must not confuse a poetry of revolution (the only Russian mistake) with a revolution of poetry. Between 1914 and 1924, France offers the spectacle of an incredible revolution in literature. 1935 initiates a new era.

Let me sleep in the sun under the sailboat lent to me by Grace of St. Once-upon-a time, a boat which I use and abuse.

I close up shop and move on. That is how peddlers take their rest.

Readers, Farewell!
Ville franche sur mer
May 1935

Notes

CHAPTER I
1. *Parade:* Ballet (1917) staged by Cocteau; music by Satie, set design by Picasso.

CHAPTER II
1. Pablo Sarasate y Navascues (1844–1908): Spanish violinist and composer.
2. Fantômas: Fictional character, the perfect criminal, subject of novelistic series, beginning in 1911, by Souvestre and Allain, and of five films (1913–1914) by Feuillade.
3. Melpomene: Greek muse of song, mother of the Sirens.
4. "The Queen's violin! The Queen's violin!"

CHAPTER III
1. Félix Mayol (1872–1941): French café-concert singer.
2. Jean Mounet-Sully (1841–1916): French actor, great interpretor of Oedipus.
3. *La Voix Humaine:* Play (1930) by Cocteau; the mademoiselles are telephone operators.
4. Léonetto Cappiello (1875–1942): Italian portraitist; Cocteau wrote the preface to the 1946 biography of Cappiello by Jacques Viénot.
5. La Saint-Charlemagne: religious holiday.
6. Hokusai (1760–1849): Japanese painter and engraver.

7. Serge Lifar (1905–?): French dancer and choreographer of Russian origin.
8. *Apollon Musagète:* Ballet (1928), music by Igor Stravinsky, choreography by Georges Balanchine, produced by Serge Diaghilev.

CHAPTER V
1. "Ta-ra-ra-boom-dee-ay, grammar gives me the sweats."

CHAPTER VI
1. Madeleine Carlier: French actress with whom Cocteau claimed to be "madly in love" and to have had an affair.
2. Zouave: French colonial infantryman, traditionally figuring as tin target at French fairground shooting galleries.
3. Swann and the Duc de Guermantes: Characters from Proust's *A la Recherche du Temps Perdu.*
4. Sidonie-Gabrielle Colette (1873–1954): French novelist.
5. Georges Goursat (pseud. Sem) (1863–1934): French society caricaturist.

CHAPTER VII
1. *Pelléas et Mélisande:* Opera (1902) by Débussy.
2. Harry Ralph (pseud. Little Titch) (1868–1928): British music-hall clown.

CHAPTER VIII
1. Fernand Crommelynk (1885–1970): Belgian playwright, author of *Le Cocu Magnifique* (1921).
2. *The Blood of a Poet:* Film (1932) by Cocteau.

CHAPTER IX
1. Alberto Santos-Dumont (1873–1932): Brazilian engineer, balloonist and aviator, holder of the first world record for a flight of 21 seconds in 1906.
2. Alfred Dreyfus (1859–1935): French Army officer falsely accused of treason in 1894 and imprisoned on Devil's Island; his defense was led by Emile Zola.

3. Jean-Louis Forain (1852–1931): French painter, designer and engraver; co-founder with Caran d'Ache of *P'sst*.
4. Emmanuel Poiré (pseud. Caran D'Ache) (1859–1909): French cartoonist and illustrator, known for his nationalist and anti-Dreyfus opinions.
5. *L'Assiette au Beurre:* French satirical weekly review founded in 1901.
6. Baron Jacques D'Adelsward-Fersen (1880–1923): French author of the scandalous *Ebauches et Débauches* (1901).
7. Félix Faure (1841–1899): French Politician; as president of the Third Republic (1895–1899) he refused to reopen the Dreyfus case.
8. Edmond Rostand (1868–1918): French poet and playwright, author of Cyrano de Bergerac (1897).
9. Julia Bartet (1854–1941): actress in the Comédie Francaise, known for her interpretations of Antigone, Andromaque and Bérénice.
10. Marie-Louise Fuller (1862–1928): American dance-hall artist.
11. Maréoramas and stéréoramas: three-dimensional topographic maps of sea and land; popular entertainments in the XIXth century.
12. René Lalique (1860–1945): French jeweller, glass-maker and designer, one of the originators of the art nouveau style.
13. Miguel Zamacois (1866–1955): French playwright.
14. Jeanne-Marie Bourgeois (pseud. Mistinquett) (1875–1956): French music-hall singer and entertainer.
15. "Yes. It's me, here I am, I'm back."
16. "They say my voice drags when I sing my song. It's true."
17. Eleonora Duse (1858–1924): Italian actress.

CHAPTER X
1. Christian Berard (1902–1949): French painter and set designer.
2. Edouard Bourdet (1887–1945): French playwright, author of *Le Sexe Faible* (1929) and *Les Temps Difficiles* (1934).
3. *L'Arlésienne:* Play (1872) by Alphonse Daudet based on his *Les Lettres de Mon Moulin* (1866), with music by Bizet.

4. Jean-Baptiste Carpeaux (1827–1875): French sculptor, designer and painter. *La Danse* (1869), sculpted for Garnier's Paris Opera House, now resides in the Louvre.
5. P. Van der Clyde (pseud. Barbette): American trapeze artist who performed in drag; later the ringmaster at Ringling Brothers Barnum and Bailey circus.

CHAPTER XI
1. Carlo Goldoni (1707–1793): Italian comic playwright.
2. Edouard de Max (1869–1924): French actor in the Comédie Francaise (1915); famous especially for his interpretations of Nero and Hamlet.
3. *Michel Strogoff:* Novel (1876) and play (1880) by Jules Verne.
4. *Les Pilules du diable:* Play (1839) by Ferdinand Laloue.

CHAPTER XII
1. Catulle Mendes (1841–1909): French writer, protegé of Gautier, early founder of the Parnassian school.
2. Ernest La Jeunesse (1874–1914): French journalist and playwright.
3. Jean de Bonnefon (1866–1928): French historian and writer.
4. Raymond Radiguet (1903–1923): French novelist, author of *Le Diable au Corps* (1923) and *Le Bal du Comte d'Orgel* (posth. 1924); Cocteau's lover.

CHAPTER XIV
1. Lucien Daudet (1883–1946): French drama critic; brother of Léon, son and biographer of Alphonse; cavalier servant to Empress Eugénie.
2. Empress Eugénia Maria de Montijo de Guzman (1826–1920), wife of Emperor Napoleon III.
3. Jules Lemaitre (1853–1914): French writer and playwright, member of the Académie Francaise (1895).
4. Léon Daudet (1868–1942): French journalist and writer, son of Alphonse Daudet; virulent right-wing founder of *L'Action Francaise*.

5. Reynaldo Hahn (1875–1947): Venezuelan composer; director of Paris Opéra (1945–47).
6. Jacques-Anatole-Francois Thibault (pseud. Anatole France) (1844–1924): French writer; recipient of Nobel Prize in 1921; supporter of Dreyfus.
7. *Le Potomak:* Novel (1919) by Cocteau.
8. Anna de Noailles (1876–1933): French poet and novelist, author of *Le Coeur Innombrable.*
9. Franz Xaver Winterhalter (1805–1873): German painter and lithographer, favorite of the court of Napoleon III and Empress Eugénie.

CHAPTER XV
1. Pauline Benda Simone (1877–?): French Actress and writer.
2. Henri Allain-Fournier (1886–1914): French novelist.
3. Charles Peguy (1873–1914): French writer and poet.
4. Jacques-Emile Blanche (1861–1942): French painter, writer, art critic; portraitist of Cocteau (1912).
5. Maurice Barres (1862–1923): French nationalist writer and politician; member of the Académie Francaise (1906).
6. Saint Thais: Egyptian courtesan of the IVth century converted by Anchorites.

CHAPTER XVI
1. Catherine Emmerich (1774–1824): German nun afflicted with stigmata who dictated her visions to the poet Clemens Brentano.
2. *Le Coq et l'Arlequin:* Pamphlet (1918) on music by Cocteau; illustrated by Picasso.
3. Jacques Chardonne (1884–1968): French novelist and essayist.
4. Edmond See (1875–1959): French playwright.
5. Sacha Guitry (1885–1957): French actor, playwright and film-maker.
6. *La Pèlerine écossaise:* Play (1950) by Sacha Guitry.
7. Paul Poiret (1879–1944): French couturier and designer, liberator of women from the traditional corset.